To My

You are not a slave
You are free
You are Blessed

Dr. Daniel Dam
08/02/23

MW01233135

NDYUKA LAND

Ndyuka Land reveals the untold story of the runaway and self-emancipated Africans in Suriname, called the Ndyuka /ənˈdʒuːkə/. The Ndyuka people represent a unique group of Maroons in Suriname. The Maroons of Suriname are the only surviving, culturally and politically autonomous, Maroon community in the world. They are the ones who have preserved the most distinctive African culture, identity, and traditions, outside of Africa.

DR. DANIEL DOMINI

"Dr. Daniel Domini has done extensive research and he has orchestrated the story of our ancestors on paper. It is an extraordinary story that must be told. While this story has been told by others in various ways, Dr. Domini did an incredible job putting it on paper for the next generation. This story must be told continuously so that the Ndyuka history will be known."

-Professor Dinguiou Tomou, Singer-songwriter, poet, researcher, lecturer, and professor of maroon languages at the University of Guyane and Amesco in Cayenne.

"Ndyuka Land is inherent to freedmen land in the hinterland of Suriname. Enslaved Africans who conquered the atrocities of slavery preserved their African heritage in governing the Ndyuka nation to date. They are socially, culturally, economically, and intellectually embedded in their preserved African "Kiya" philosophy and literacy for life."

- Fidelia Graand-Galon, Ph.D., Ambassador of the Republic of Suriname to Ghana

NDYUKA LAND

Copyright © 2022 by Dr. Daniel Domini

All rights reserved. No part of this book may be used or reproduced by any means, graphic, electronic, or mechanical, including photocopying, recording, taping, or by any information storage retrieval system, without the written permission of the publisher except in the case of brief quotations embodied in critical articles and reviews.

Hardcover ISBN: 979-8-9852557-0-6

All images in this book are originals taken by the author for this book or recreated versions of existing images of certain historic figures. The author owns all rights to these images and reserves all rights.

Ndyuka Warrior

Ndyuka written in the Afaka syllabary

ABSTRACT

The Ndyuka /ənˈdʒuːkə/ Land book is a historical and cultural endeavor aimed at educating the world about the untold story of the runaway and self-emancipated Africans in Suriname and how their faith and resilience played an essential part in their lives. This book became an internal journey, and with that, a necessity to share my story with the world – to uncover my tribal history and unleash my ancestral voice. I studied the ancestors of my homeland and the Ndyuka tribe, in addition to visiting Ndyuka villages in the interior of Suriname, and spending many years immersed in the culture of the indigenous people, visiting elders within multiple villages, and sitting with historians to learn more about the Ndyuka tribe.

The Ndyuka Land book illustrates an intimate encounter with my lineage and roots. The pursuit of the Ndyuka Land book was not only sought for historical perspective but to understand the Ndyuka people's immeasurable faith in God expressed by their ancestors in such a tremendous way and their resiliency to fight for their freedom.

Within this book, you will also begin to learn of Malogassi, which symbolizes the complete embodiment of the warrior spirit embedded and thriving within the Ndyuka people. Malogassi is most depicted within the life and conquests of Boni, the Ndyuka Warrior. Within all of us, there is an inner warrior, derived from the fight of our ancestors. The warrior that seeks to understand more, the warrior that endlessly pursues justice, and the warrior fervently breaking the chains of generational curses, physical and mental bondage, and societal oppression. Malogassi represents fortitude from experience, aggressiveness in purpose, fervent faith, and communal strength. I AM MALOGASSI.

As a result of this book, I was able to connect with community leaders to help improve their community and social platform. The Ndyuka Land book is a powerful resource tool for those who are interested in expanding their knowledge in the field of African studies or for individuals attempting to gain a greater understanding of the Ndyuka tribe in Suriname and the Trans-Atlantic slave business, particularly the slaves in South America and Suriname. Finally, the Ndyuka knowledge will allow researchers from various fields to broaden their vocabulary in cultural competency, minority relations, spiritual fortitude, and community leadership.

BOOK DEDICATION

I dedicate this book to my Ndyuka tribe; the Maroons in Suriname and the Diaspora worldwide. To all runaway slaves who fled the horrors of slavery, your cries were heard, and your story will never be forgotten. To all who fought the colonial system of oppression, I embody your sweat and tears, and I continue to carry the gauntlet that pursues racial equality and cultural liberation. To those still fighting forms of modern-day slavery, injustice, sex trafficking, and forced child labor, may this book serve as a roadmap to justice, a referendum for reform, and an exposé of any oppression that still seeks to cripple society in this 21st century. Finally, to all who are still seeking mental, emotional, and spiritual freedom, may the words of these pages bring you a sense of healing, therapeutic identity, and inward transformation.

ACKNOWLEDGMENTS

In composing this book, I have been privileged to ingest the knowledge of several subject matter experts, historians, and cultural icons to create the transcendent narratives that flow through the chapters of this literary work. A special thank you to my father, Tribal Elder Alfons Domini (Baa Nya Nyang), and my uncles Petrus Domini (Agasang) and historian, André R.M. Pakosie, for their deep understanding and enlightenment of the Maroon culture. Their foresight into the value of restorative justice, coupled with their informative insight, historical research, and personal experiences added great value to the Ndyuka story. I would also like to offer a heart of gratitude to the history narrators of Suriname, Tribal Elder Da Kofi Jojo, Tribal Elder Robbert Asoiti, and Jacques Atiaso Isak. Thank you for your lifelong commitment to keeping the Ndyuka story alive for generations to come.

CONTENTS

LIST OF FIGURES

Figure 1 Fort Zeelandia in Paramaribo, Suriname

INTRODUCTION

We are all complex people. As a Surinamese American of African descent, I share the history of slavery and racism in the United States. Similarly, as a product of African tribal systems, I share my identity with the place of my ancestors. More specifically, I share the location and identity of my tribe in what is modernly known as Suriname. Like the United States, Suriname was built upon the capturing and selling of African men, women, and children into slavery. In July 2017, I revisited Fort Zeelandia, a prominent place in the capital of Suriname, where European slave traders transported slaves (among them my ancestors) from West Africa to Suriname.

This literary work will describe and share the story of slavery and Suriname based on my research and my ancestral history. The continued effects of slavery in the United States will be looked at through the lens of my people, the Ndyuka, who were able to escape from slavery and create a social, economic, and political structure that continues to exist to this day in Suriname. In order to have hope, we must look at the narratives that lie outside of our common understanding, narratives of beginnings that speak to who we are and where we come from, and narratives of survival, heroism, and community.

Figure 2 Fort Zeelandia in Paramaribo, Suriname

I am concerned that many people in the United States and around the world do not know the story of the "Bush Negroes" or "Maroons," also known as the Ndyuka people in Suriname, South America. I am compelled to share my tribe's story with the world so all may know that while slave traders captured and sold millions of people into slavery, some people managed to flee the horrors of slavery and maintain their freedom. This book will encourage people from the diaspora whose ancestors were enslaved and those who experienced any form of oppression and injustice by illustrating my ancestors' faith, endurance, resilience, intelligence, and intuitiveness.

HOW TO APPROACH THIS BOOK

I consider this an essential work of the Ndyuka people. My upbringing in Paramaribo, Suriname, and regular visits with my parents to my Ndyuka village on the Cottica and Marowijne River have prepared me for a lifetime of research on the Ndyuka or Maroon people from Suriname, which I'm a part of. My theological and historical research has given me a greater love and appreciation for my people. Within my culture as a Ndyuka, written resources and culture in earlier periods are scarce due to Ndyuka people believing that they should keep their knowledge only amongst themselves; therefore, creating internal history narrators. I use the term history narrators because most of these Ndyuka people could not read or write, and consequently, they were trained from early childhood to have a sharp memory.

Their history is passed from one generation to the next, and a particular group of elders among them would serve as their go-to person for all the historical details of their ancestry. These elders were like history books. These elders trained children and young adults with a natural gift of mental aptitude and sharpness to become historical experts. I was only 7 years old when my daddy would take my twin brother and me to Elder Da Kofi (Da Jojo), my daddy's uncle, who was revered as a historical narrator in the community. In my 7-year-old mind, I saw Da Kofi as a tall, bony, coffee-brown man...not the most attractive man. I could not tell whether Da Kofi was sick in one leg or if his leg was amputated, but one thing I knew was that he walked with an unusual limp. At the rise of dawn each Saturday, my daddy would go to Da Kofi's house, a broken-down house filled with eclectic, uncommon furniture pieces. You would see traditional wooden carved benches that were frequently uncomfortable to sit on, with no seat cushions for comfort...just a hard bench, with no back support.

Figure 3 Wooden Traditional Carved Bench

As far back as I can remember, I do not think Da Kofi had proper electricity. Whether he had electricity or not, there were moments when he would light either a candle or an old lamp and begin, as I call it, his history class. Da Kofi had a systematic way of conveying his message to my dad. It was in a form that, even as a child, you could retain and memorize the words he brought forth. Da Kofi got his story from the late Gaanman or King of the Ndyuka people, Akontu Velanti, who ruled from 1950 to 1964.[1] Da Kofi would convey the message with great honor, respect, and reference to Gaanman Akontu Velanti. In every sentence, it seemed as though he would say verbatim what he heard from Gaanman Akontu Velanti. With each line of oral history, he would either start or end his statement with "Akontu Velanti." For example, he would begin by saying, "Da (respected father) Akontu Velanti said so," and then he would state the historical fact, or at

---

[1] Wilhelmina van Velzen and H.U.E. Thoden van Velzen, "Suriname: Een Wingewest Van De Republiek," *Een Zwarte Vrijstaat in Suriname (Deel 2)*, no. 32 (2013): pp. 53-64, https://doi.org/10.1163/9789004255494_004.

4

the end of the sentence, he would say, "Just like Da Akontu Velanti said." Da Kofi would continue this practice for the duration of the lesson.

In my book, you will find intense research on both the documented and oral history of the Ndyuka people. After careful consideration, the oral history that I will be presenting in my book will be transcribed from my encounters with Da Kofi.

In approaching this book, it is imperative to grasp the concept of paper research versus oral history. The paper research is based on the books and references that tell the story of the Ndyuka people, but there have been only a few studies of this single maroon society called "The Ndyuka." Therefore, since the Ndyuka traditionally did not share many of their stories, I, as a Ndyuka myself, will share oral stories from reliable sources that were untold in the past. The paper study is according to scholarly standards, but the oral history of the Ndyuka people is equal to, if not transcendent above, paper accounts, because who would be able to describe their story better than the Ndyuka themselves, giving firsthand accounts of their history. One of the main reasons why the history of the Ndyuka people was not written was because they emancipated themselves from slavery and fled into the jungle, where there was no one literate and capable of capturing their history on paper. As a result, they put a system in place of preserving their history by passing it on orally from one generation to the next.

This book aims for people to feel liberated and genuinely happy when they read this book. It also aims for people to feel free, and to have hope. It is crucial, in reading this book, to note that this book is not intended as a way to mourn slavery, but to bring awareness to the fact that, while other nations and people were enslaved, there was a minority group that stood up and fought for their rights. As you approach the pages of this literary masterpiece, view it from a lens of seeking wholeness, freedom, and justice, not vengeance.

Figure 4 Ndyuka Man Working in the Village

CHAPTER 1

SURINAME: THE FORGOTTEN GEM OF THE CARIBBEAN

Transatlantic Slave Trade in Ghana

"Den gaawan taki, efu yu sabi fu lon, yu mu sabi fu kibii"

(The elders told us, "If you know how to run, you must know how to hide)

[Ndyuka proverb]

On the coast of the Atlantic Ocean lies Fort Elmina. This port served for 200 years as a mecca for transatlantic slavery. From this slave depot, the Dutch transported thousands of African slaves to South America, the Caribbean, and the United States in slave ships under inhumane conditions. During the 16th century, the Dutch were very ambitious and looking for different opportunities to make a name for themselves as a young nation.

Figure 5 Fort Elmina in Ghana

There was stiff competition between the Netherlands, the Spanish, and the Portuguese monarchies. Although they were all established kingdoms, the Spaniards and the Portuguese were far more advanced than the up-and-coming Netherlands. In 1568, as a thriving nation, the Netherlands believed itself to be vibrant and strong, leading to the Dutch revolt and war with the Spanish and Portuguese, nations considered to be much tougher.

Figure 6 Fort Elmina Courtyard in Ghana

The Spaniards and the Portuguese were world leaders during this era. They were world conquerors and knew the entire coast of Brazil since the 1500s. In the 1540s, the Portuguese started to colonize parts of the coast of Brazil, and they began to experiment with the production of sugarcane, cacao, and coffee.[2] At the same time, the Portuguese started using the Indians, the indigenous people of the land, as slaves for their cacao, sugarcane, and coffee crop and harvesting. Hence, both the Spaniards and the Portuguese started experimenting with sugarcane; they became greedy and wanted to realize great wealth in the industry like the world majority. They quickly discovered that sugar was the new gold. The Portuguese soon discovered that the Indian slaves working the fields were not immune to the different diseases brought by the Europeans to South America as they began to witness the Indians die in immense measure. Death reached an excruciatingly high toll, forcing the European colonizers to look for laborers elsewhere...Africa. Back in the Netherlands, the greed for money or the pursuit

---

[2] John H. Elliott, *Spain, Europe & the Wider World, 1500-1800* (New Haven, CT: Yale University Press, 2009).

thereof was the critical focus. Thus, although the Spaniards and the Portuguese were enemies of the Netherlands, the Netherlands copied their slave practices and how they handled the slave business.[3] One of the biggest desires of the Netherlands was to conquer Brazil. As their greed for power and money ensued, the Netherlands finally began to plot their strategy to overcome their competition. For the Netherlands to conquer Brazil, they founded the West India Company (WIC). The purpose of the West India Company was to destroy or eradicate the Spaniards and the Portuguese. To accomplish this feat, the Netherlands invested large amounts of money into this plot, and within 7 years, they were able to conquer part of Brazil. The West India Company was successful, not only in South America but also in other parts of the world. In Ghana, Africa, the West India Company was also able to conquer Fort Elmina from the Spaniards, a fort used by the Spaniards to conduct slave business, and consequently, assumed ownership of the profitable slave business.[4]

After accomplishing their mission to eradicate the Spaniards and the Portuguese, along with the new acquisition of the fort, the West India Company decided to focus solely on slave acquisition and sale. The company based its headquarters in Fort Elmina, on the coast of Ghana, with the support of two big multinational companies, Shell and Phillips. Soon this became the center of business exchange. They were doing business in ivory, gold, and slave exchange. Slavery existed in Africa long before the Europeans arrived in the 1500s. Meanwhile, the slave business was booming in South America, and the West India Company did not want to put money into the Dutch colonies in North America and places like the New Netherlands, which later became known as New York. As

---

[3] Pieter C. Emmer, "The History of the Dutch Slave Trade, A Bibliographical Survey," *The Journal of Economic History* 32, no. 3 (1972): pp. 728-747, https://doi.org/10.1017/s0022050700077214.

[4] Minchinton, Walter. "The Dutch in the Atlantic Slave Trade: 1600-1815." *The English Historical Review* 109, no. 431 (1994): 454+. *Gale Literature Resource Center* (accessed March 21, 2022).

a result, England started conquering Dutch territories in the north, including New York, which was a Dutch colony. After England defeated the New Netherlands, there was a peace treaty between the Netherlands and England. In this peace treaty, England decided to trade New York with Suriname, meaning that England would keep New Netherlands (which is New York), and since Suriname was an English colony, they decided to give that to the Dutch as a consolation prize.[5] Having such a beautiful paradise in the Caribbean would serve as a gift to the Dutch. The geographical setting of Suriname is unique because Suriname is part of South America and part of the Caribbean.

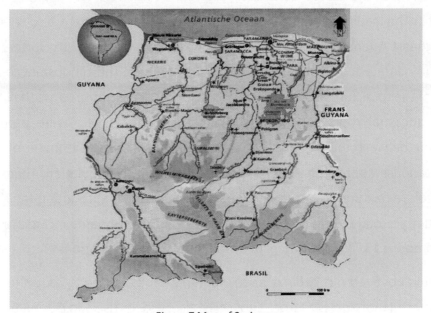

Figure 7 Map of Suriname

Suriname is a lovely country, a sovereign state that lies on the Northeastern parts of the Atlantic coast of South America. It is one of the smallest countries in South America, initially inhabited by the indigenous tribesmen before the 16th century when it was first explored by the Spaniards and later settled in by the English towards the mid-17th century. The Dutch colonized Suriname in 1667. In

---

[5] John Paxton, *The Statesman's Year-Book: Statistical and Historical Annual of the States of the World for the Year* (London: Macmillan, 1976).

1863, African slavery was abolished, and migrant workers were brought from India and Indonesia, namely Java, to settle in Suriname. In 1975, Suriname attained its independence from the Dutch colony and elected a civilian government. However, it maintained its close economic, diplomatic, and cultural ties to its colonizer. This, perhaps, explains why Suriname is the only sovereign state outside of Europe where much of its citizenry uses the Dutch language.[6]

Suriname is one of the most ethnically diverse countries in the Americas. Most of its populace descended from the African slaves and Indians, as well as the Javanese, who the Dutch colonizers brought in to work on their agricultural projects.[7] The leading ethnic group in Suriname is the Hindustani, also referred to as Southeast Asian, whose ancestral background can be traced to Northern India and who migrated to Suriname in the late 19th century. The Hindustani constitute 27.4% of the total Surinamese population. The second ethnic group is the Maroon, whose ancestral roots can be traced to African slaves who were brought to Suriname between the 17th and 18th centuries, before the abolishment of slavery. They comprise approximately 21.7% of the Surinamese population. There is also the Creole, a mixture of Whites and Blacks in the country, accounting for 15.7% of the country's total population. Other ethnic groups in Suriname include Javanese, who comprise 13.7%, and others in unspecified ethnic formations.[8]

The above ethnic groups speak different local dialects, but the official Surinamese language is Dutch. English is also widely used in Suriname. Other ethnic languages include Sranan Tongo, also referred to as Taki-Taki, which is a lingua franca used by the Creole ethnic group and younger populations. Sarnami

---

[6] Central Intelligence Agency. *The World Factbook 2016-17*, 50th ed. (Washington, D.C.: Central Intelligence Agency, 2016).

[7] "Suriname Country Profile," BBC News (BBC, March 3, 2021), https://www.bbc.com/news/world-latin-america-19997673.

[8] Central Intelligence Agency. "The World Factbook," last modified 2021, https://www.cia.gov/the-world-factbook/..

Hindustani is spoken by the Hindustani, which is a variant of the Bhojpuri language, and Javanese Surinamese is the language spoken by the Javanese.[9]

In terms of religion, a 23.6% majority of Surinamese are Protestants, followed by Hinduism at 22.3%, Roman Catholic at 21.6%, Muslim at 13.8%, and several forms of Christianity at 3.2%, including Jehovah's Witness at 1.2%. The remaining are unspecified.[10]

Demographic Profile of Suriname

Suriname has a pluralistic population composed primarily of Creoles, including a mixture of African and European backgrounds. The Maroon ethnic group is descended from African slaves who were settled in Suriname after the abolition of slavery. The Javanese ethnic group is composed of the Indian and Indonesian contract workers who settled in Suriname. Generally, Suriname is in a post-industrial demographic transition, having a low fertility rate within the non-Maroon population, a relatively low mortality rate, and a rising life expectancy rate. These statistics are slightly different for the Maroon ethnic group living in the rural areas of the country. They have low access to education and contraceptives, higher levels of malnutrition, minimal access to electricity and piped water, insufficient sanitation, poor infrastructure, and inadequate healthcare.

During the 19th century, well-educated Surinamese who mainly spoke the Dutch language began migrating to the Netherlands, Suriname's colonizer, with approximately 350,000 still residing there to date. Although disrupted by World War II, emigration continued to meet the increased demand for labor in the

---

[9] Robert David Borges, "The Life of Language: Dynamics of Language Contact in Suriname," 2014.

[10] "World Factbook (Statistics Are Also Based on 2012 Estimates)," *Central Intelligence Agency*, https://www.cia.gov/the-world-factbook/countries/world/.

Netherlands after the war's conclusion. Most of these emigrants were ethnic Creoles who predominantly used the Dutch language.[11]

Suriname's ties with the Netherlands are not only influenced by economic and political factors but also social, as most Surinamese have relatives living in the Netherlands. The Netherlands is also the greatest supplier of Surinamese development aid. In essence, the Netherlands has experienced the largest Surinamese migration to date, closely followed by French Guiana, the United States, and the Caribbean. Subsequently, Suriname has also seen a large influx of international migration. Suriname has weak immigration laws making it easy for one to enter the country illegally. The rain forests that obscure its borders are an advantage to illegal immigrants. Since the mid-1980s, Brazilians have been living in Paramaribo, Suriname's capital, and east Suriname, where they engage in mining gold as their main economic activity.[12] The intense immigration of Brazilians and other communities in South America is orienting the country to its Latin American roots.

Suriname is largely characterized by a youthful population with the country's population between 0 and 14 years being at 24.11% and those between 15 and 24 years comprising 17.36% of the country's total population. A vast majority of the Surinamese population are between 25 and 54 years old, estimated to be 44.42% of the country's total population. Those between 55 and 65 years old represent only 7.94% of the country's total population. The country has a small aging population comprising only 6.17% of Suriname's total population.[13] This

---

[11] Hans van Amersfoort, "Oxford University Research Archive," (University of Oxford, October 2011), https://ora.ox.ac.uk/objects/uuid:d71958a0-7fe7-4809-b635-1e468cfb96a1/download_file?file_format=pdf&safe_filename=WP47%2BHow%2Bthe%2BDutch%2BGovernment.pdf&type_of_work=Working+paper.

[12] Wim Hoogbergen and Dirk Kruijt, "Gold, 'Garimpeiros' and Maroons: Brazilian Migrants and ...," Caribbean Studies (Institute of Caribbean Studies, 2004), https://www.jstor.org/stable/25613440.

[13] Central Intelligence Agency. "World Factbook (Statistics Are Based on 2018 Estimates)," last modified 2021, https://www.cia.gov/the-world-factbook/countries/world/.

indicates that many of the people in Suriname are relatively young and productive. However, as indicated above, the improving life expectancy may slightly alter these statistics as the upper age groups will significantly improve from the current low figures.

Overview of Suriname's Economy

Suriname is a country endowed with natural resources, including large mineral reserves, forests for timber, and other rich endowments in fishing, agriculture, and industry. Suriname has all it needs to be a prosperous country, but many years of military misrule and other forms of political turbulence have taken a toll to the extent that the country is struggling to turn its national resources into wealth its countrymen can enjoy.[14]

For a long time, the Surinamese economy has relied on sugarcane, which the Dutch introduced in the 17th century. The sugar plantations played a major role in the current ethnic composition of Suriname as most Surinamese are African, Indian, and Javanese laborers who were working in these sugar plantations. As the country gained its independence, the sugar plantations were abandoned, and by the 20th century, the core economic activity was bauxite mining and processing. This was the major industry. To date, bauxite mining and processing contributes up to 70% of the country's export revenue.[15] However, geological surveys do not give this industry a long life as most of the old mines have been exhausted. In order to continue mining bauxite, there is a need for fresh exploration and

---

[14] Scott B. MacDonald, "Suriname's Economic Crisis," Center for Strategic and International Studies, April 20, 2017, https://www.csis.org/analysis/surinames-economic-crisis.

[15] D.A. Monsels, "Bauxite Deposits in Suriname: Geological Context and Resource Development: Netherlands Journal of Geosciences," Cambridge Core (Cambridge University Press, March 17, 2016), https://core-cms.prod.aop.cambridge.org/core/journals/netherlands-journal-of-geosciences/article/bauxite-deposits-in-suriname-geological-context-and-resource-development/CF28E3F7ECAA5BA0EBCC34334CDEF257.

development of new mines, but with the current infrastructural inadequacies, this continues to be a problematic strategy.[16]

The country grapples with uneven distribution of infrastructural development, most of which is concentrated along the narrow coastal plain, leaving the interior portion of the country, which is the largest area, largely underdeveloped and therefore inaccessible. Moreover, the Surinamese government is not in complete control of this area. The low level of development and subsequent inaccessibility makes exploitation of natural resource reserves like oil, gold, kaolin, stones, and timber very difficult and expensive. Given that this is a vast area, statistics indicate that the Surinamese natural resource sector has a lot of potential but remains largely underdeveloped.[17]

Political uncertainty and resource mismanagement by the country's leadership has been the country's impediment to attaining economic prosperity. In 1982, the Netherlands, which was and is still the country's benefactor, cut off aid to the military junta leading to further economic deterioration of the country. In a bid to stabilize the country's economy, a structural adjustment program was initiated in 1992 with strategies like improved tax collection, revocation of some government subsidies, and harmonization of exchange rates. Although this went a long way towards curbing the country's soaring inflation by bringing it down from 400% in 1994 to less than 1% in 1996, the country failed to implement more difficult reforms such as trimming the bloated civil service and privatizing key government-owned industries that were largely inefficient. Fueled by the absence of a clear and progressive economic plan, the Surinamese inflation rate soared in the late 1990s, initiating its currency's woes as it began to tumble.[18]

---

[16] MacDonald, "Suriname's Economic Crisis."

[17] Richard M. Auty, Natural Resources and Economic Development: Two Stylized Facts Models (Helsinki, 2000).

[18] United Nations, Preliminary Overview of the Economies of Latin America and the Caribbean 2017 (Washington D.C.: United Nations Economic Commission for Latin America and the Caribbean, 2018).

Moving into the 21st century, Suriname's leading economy has been focused on the mining industry, with the export of gold and oil accounting for approximately 85% of exports and 27% of government revenues. Suriname's economy is in a state of vulnerability at this moment, mainly because of the worldwide drop in mineral and international commodity prices, which has caused the country to experience a significant loss of revenue. Additionally, in November 2015, a major U.S. aluminum company discontinued its mining activities in Suriname.[19] This company had been operating in mining for 99 years. This has caused the public revenue to fall significantly together with export, international reserves, employment, and private sector investment. After the election of 2020, with the new government coming in, there is much anticipation that incoming leadership will stabilize the economy and create an atmosphere of prosperity. However, it remains uncertain because the government's commitment to reform the banking sector and reform the economy may not be effective without pressure from the International Monetary Fund (IMF). Suriname remains one of the largest providers of natural resources.

---

[19] Central Intelligence Agency, The CIA World Factbook 2011 (New York: Skyhorse Publishing, 2010).

CHAPTER 2

THE WEST MEETS THE WEST

The Beginning of New World Racism: Pre-European Slavery in Africa

MALOGASSI

"Pe go de, naanda kon baka de"

(Wherever I am going, from there I will return)

Before the onset of the European slave trade business, millions of slaves were captured by Arabs and taken through the Sahara to Arabic countries such as Morocco and Algeria. Slavery in Africa was in existence long before the arrival of the Europeans.[20] For example, if you owed somebody money, and you were unable to pay your debt, a member of your household would work for your debtor until you could pay them back in full. If you could not oblige, that person would continue to work, or the person that you owed would sell that person to get his or her money back. This human property could be your son or your daughter, indebted as a sacrifice unto your debtor until you could pay, at which point they would then be released.

The Dynamics of African Slave Captivity by Slave Traders

The Africans would go after each other and sell these Africans to the White or European slave traders for guns, gun powder, and other types of materials. They would capture their fellow Africans on the field or farm during the day in plain daylight or at night and take fathers, mothers, daughters, and sons. Sometimes, they were so ruthless as to take the entire household. Meanwhile, the ship would remain offshore as the captured Africans would be transported to the ship. However, there have also been depictions stating that the Whites or the Europeans never went onto African soil to catch the Africans. Still, history shows that some of these Whites indeed went into the jungle and African villages to capture these Africans and take them into slavery, doing so with major cruelty. When the slave traders, mainly the West India Company, caught the slaves, they would check the

---

[20] "Genetic Impact of African Slave Trade Revealed in DNA Study," BBC News (BBC, July 24, 2020), https://www.bbc.com/news/world-africa-53527405.

Africans first, before purchase or sale, to ensure that they were healthy and fit enough to go through the journey.

If the potential slaves met their standards, at that moment, they would buy the slave who was either captured or bought directly from fellow Africans, brand them with fire, chain them, and keep them locked in captivity at Fort Elmina until they had an ample number of African slaves for transport to North America, South America, and the Caribbean. At times, it could take several months of captivity in the fort before transportation. During this time, the level of cruelty against the Africans was unbearable and inhumane. The situation was so deplorable that they lacked basic food and water supply, locked up in masses for months in one cell where they didn't see the light of day. Additionally, there was no proper sanitation, no running water, and no bathroom facilities for use. Without a bathroom, the slaves released all urine and feces on the floor below them. One can only imagine the stench in a room or cell that held approximately 300-400 people at a time. At night there was no light, just pure darkness, and during the day, the heat could reach up to 90 degrees, and in the sun, once the cell door was shut, temperatures could rise well over 100 degrees Fahrenheit with no ventilation.[21]

Figure 8 Waiting Cell

---

[21] Sawh Ruth and Alice M. Scales, "Middle Passage in the Triangular Slave Trade: The West Indies," Negro Educational Review 57, no. 3/4 (2006): 155–170.

To make matters worse, the Africans were beaten if the slave traders were not pleased with their actions. In later years, archaeologists went back to dig up floor samples of the slave cells to study the ground materials and discovered that the smooth tar-like sections that resembled pavement were remnants of African slave feces left on the floor from centuries ago.

Figure 9 Pavement Shows Remnants of African Slave Feces Left on the Floor from Centuries Ago.

At the fort, before the slave trader would ship the slaves to North and South America and the Caribbean, they would put a burn mark on them with the slave company or modern-day broker of ownership. The burn process was a cast iron with the initials of the company; for example, "WI" would represent West India Company, and the initials would be placed on the African's back, using cast iron placed on heat until it was scolding red. This was to help to identify who the rightful owner of a slave was.

Figure 10 Cast Iron with the Slave Company Initials for Burn Mark

Figure 11 The Infamous Door of No Return at Fort Elmina in Ghana

After going through all these inhumane situations at the fort, it would be fair to assume that this was the end of the struggle and cruelty. However, once the Africans were taken to the ship, a ship doctor would thoroughly examine them before setting sail, as there were special criteria for becoming a slave.[22] The qualifications to become a slave were as follows: a male should be between the ages of 15 and 35 years old, and they were not allowed to have any grey hair. You

---

[22] Gysbert de Witt et al., *Verhandelingen Uitgegeven Door Het Zeeuwsch Genootschap Der Wetenschappen Te Vlissingen: [Volume 1]*, 1st ed. (Middelburg : P. Gillissen, Leiden, 1769).

had to be physically strong and not show any signs of fever or any disease or any sign of weakness. According to the ship doctor's diagnosis, if you were not healthy enough, the slave traders would send the Africans back to land or throw them into the water and leave them for dead. It was said that some of these kidnapped Africans looked sick, but the truth of the matter was that they were so terrified that their countenance changed to reflect that of illness. Some were further terrified because they thought they would be killed, and that the White people would eat them.

Life on the Slave Ships

A ship could carry up to 750 Africans, and the trip could last for up to two months. The slave traders would pack the slaves at the bottom of the ship, using every single space allotted on the vessel. This made life on the ship deplorable and dangerous. It was worse than when they were being held in the fort temporarily.

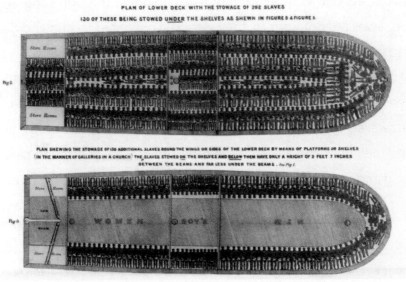

Figure 12 The Famous Picture by Brookes Shows How They Transported the Africans

One of the famous pictures by Brookes shows how they transported the Africans.[23] The space on the ship was designed to fit one body. The space provided for each man was 6 feet by 1 foot 4 inches, with the women and children having slightly less room, and on top of that, a slave was chained by their ankles and neck. Historians state that the space was the exact dimensions as that of a standard casket. There was no sanitation on the ship for the kidnapped Africans to use, no bathroom, no toilet, meaning that one of the kidnapped Africans could stay up to 4 months in the dungeon on the fort, and 2 months on the ship, going 3-6 months without bathing. These deplorable conditions caused many to lose their lives. The slaves were on their own, no one was on their side, and no one helped them. They would rebel against the slave traders from time to time, and they would either get killed or get horrible punishment. The appalling situation on the ship caused some of the slaves to lose their lives, and those that died or were killed were thrown overboard.

While they were on the ship, the slave traders would occasionally bring the captured Africans out to stretch themselves, doing so through song and dance. Even if the slaves did not want to, they were still obligated to sing and dance, as it was vital to the slave capturers and good for business if the Africans stayed fit and healthy.[24] No one wanted to purchase a sick slave. As such, they would let the Africans dance for hours so they could stay in shape. While they were dancing and singing; however, they were still in shackles and never released from the shackles that bound their neck and ankles. If the captured Africans refused to participate in the dancing and singing, they were beaten and even killed. The captured Africans were constantly rebelling against the harsh treatment. Even though they did not

---

[23] Stowage of the British Slave Ship "Brookes" under the Regulated Slave Trade Act of 1788, Printed Ephemera Collection (Library of Congress) DLC (Great Britain Liverpool: Library of Cogress, 1788), https://www.loc.gov/item/98504459/.

[24] Alan Rice, "Revealing Histories: Remembering Slavery," Legacies of slavery: dance | Revealing Histories, accessed March 27, 2022, http://revealinghistories.org.uk/legacies-stereotypes-racism-and-the-civil-rights-movement/articles/legacies-of-slavery-dance.html.

have anyone to fight for them, they fought for themselves because the cruelty on the ship was unbearable.

Figure 13 Example of Slave Ship Heading to The Caribbean

In the late 1800s, on the coast of Suriname, these captured Africans were able to conquer the ship.[25] The ship crew jumped in the water, and the Africans escaped to dry land to a place unknown. I believe these people were the Ndyukas.

The Million Dollar Question: Why did the Europeans Treat the Slaves in Such a Cruel Way?

Unless we find the correct and satisfactory answer to this gruesome question, we will always wonder why the Europeans treated the Africans with such cruelty. In modern times, we may also ask why did the Whites treat the Blacks with such disregard for their dignity? We must understand the origin of the investigation of this heinous act against a fellow human being. The question is, why would one treat their fellow human being with such hatred or disregard? Why would one group see themselves as superior to another group, particularly the Whites to the Blacks? Why would a White person see themselves as superior? In 1768, Dutch

---

[25] Allison Blakely, "Historical Ties among Suriname, the Netherlands Antilles, Aruba, and the Netherlands," *Callaloo* 21, no. 3 (1998): pp. 472-478, https://doi.org/10.1353/cal.1998.0135.

anatomist, Petrus Camper, conducted research in the Netherlands, and his research revealed that in opening up the Negro's brain, he had a normal brain, his skin was normal as any other White being, and in looking at the Negro's blood, it was red like any other White being. Hence, in Camper's findings, he stated that although the Negro had a dark complexion on the outside, different from the white complexion, on the inside, the Negro was the same as a White person. In his findings, he also determined that Blacks and Whites are physiologically equal, both internally and externally. Years before Camper's research, the Germans had done their research on the Negro or Black person as well, and their findings were completely different from the Dutch. In their findings, it was reported that in opening a Negro's brain, they found that the brain was black, under the skin of the Negro was black, and the blood was black; therefore, the Negro must not have been human, but a mixture of animal and human species. In this case, they deemed it a mixture of White humans and apes; therefore, the Black individual was seen as a human-ape, unequal and inferior to their White counterparts.[26] According to such rationale of the Whites, or in this case, the slave trader, since the Black people were mixed with animals, they were to be seen as animals and treated accordingly.

The Beginning of New World Racism: The West Meets the West

The White Europeans flocked to the Gold Coast as word spread quickly in the Netherlands that there was a new standard of quick money to be made by capturing and selling the Africans to the plantations in both North America and South America, namely Suriname. Many businesspeople took government loans to invest in the slave business, and a large number of Europeans left Europe to go

---

[26] Bob Moore, Nierop Henk F K van, and Angelie Sens, "Dutch Debates on Overseas Man and His World, 1770-1820," in *Colonial Empires Compared: Britain and the Netherlands, 1750-1850: Papers Delivered to the Fourteenth Anglo-Dutch Historical Conference, 2000*, 1st ed. (Aldershot, Hampshire, England: Ashgate, 2003), pp. 77-93.

to the Gold Coast in Ghana.[27] Here we see where the west meets the west. For many of these White Europeans, it was all about the greed to make quick money. They did not care about how they made the money, and whose lives would be cut short; all that mattered was for them to make as much as they could and get rich quickly. The original plan was to make the money, go back to Europe, and live large.

You can imagine the anticipation they had going to the new world to find the hot commodities in Africa. For many, upon arrival, that dream of getting rich quickly was shattered because they experienced a different scenario. They were flabbergasted by what they saw. For many of them, it was their first time seeing Black people and people with different skin color than their own. They saw people who painted their faces and spoke a completely different dialect. People who were half-naked, living and going about their business, living their lives, and enjoying nature. They saw hard-working people, people with their families, and people who were responsible. Unfortunately, the greed to accomplish their goal at any cost did not stop them from disturbing the peaceful lives that the Black people lived. The Europeans also discovered quickly that the get-rich-quick idea or intention was not so easily attainable. They discovered that there was no magical solution to wealth because the slave business did not yield a quick return. They learned that they had to wait on the fort for months to get these Africans in, and then, in turn, the Africans would have to wait there for up to 3 months until the slave traders gathered enough human merchandise to fill a ship. At which point, the slave traders would then sail to North or South America for another 3 to 4 months, sell the Africans upon arrival to work on the plantation, produce the crops, and in turn sell the crops for profit.[28] Their greed quickly turned into discouragement and

---

[27] Johannes Postma, *The Dutch in the Atlantic Slave Trade, 1600-1815* (Cambridge: Cambridge Univ. Press, 2008).

[28] Joseph K. Adjaye, *Elmina, 'the Little Europe': European Impact and Cultural Resilience* (Legon-Accra: Sub-Saharan Publishers, 2018).

disappointment because they realized that the investment put into the slave business would not pay off as fast as they thought.

Many of them invested everything to come to West Africa. Some could not handle the weather and were not immune to many of the diseases that were present in Africa, resulting in numerous premature deaths. Some became sick from illnesses such as malaria, spread by the anopheles mosquito, and yellow fever, spread by the Aedes aegypti mosquito.[29] They were often lonely and bitter and even suffered from mental decapitation resulting in insanity. They were angry at themselves, and they took that anger out on their staff, in addition to the Africans. They would threaten their workers, and at times even throw spears at them. There would be moments of chaos at the West India Company's office. Furthermore, you could imagine the disposition of those captured Africans with their fate in the hands of people with such mental turmoil. The situation became so detrimental at one point that the leaders of the West India Company headquarters in Ghana turned to alcoholism.

Two said leaders were Willem Bosman and Willem Van Vogenbrock. Van Vogenbrock had so much hatred in him that he would not only degrade his own staff at the West India Company office, but because of his great disdain for the Africans, he did not hesitate to inflict his wrath upon Black men and women. Before he started expressing his animosity towards Black men and women, he always wanted to make sure he expressed his praise and satisfaction toward White women. As he said, White women were beautiful, slender, fine, well-educated, and pure because they were White. He believed White women received power from the "most high," as their god saw everything.

---

[29] Elena Esposito, Side Effects of Immunities: The African Slave Trade, Economics Working Papers, 2015.

Figure 14 Willem Bosman

Willem Bosman also did not hold back on his feelings towards the Blacks. He described all Black men as "niggers," being schematic, evil, cheeky, and untrustworthy. He also characterized them as unbelievably lazy, unimaginably carefree, and devious.[30] Van Vogenbrock also described Black women as niggers and mulatto women who were seen as a subject of amusement. He said they were deadly creatures, unashamed, desperate, and the most ungodly form of ugliness. Van Vogenbrock went so far as to say, "Even if he were a dog, he would not piss on them."[31] Interestingly, he would express his admiration and divinity for White women while degrading Black women. Many considered this as the beginning of new world racism. As I see it, this was the beginning of new world racism, where the western world met West Africa and where the White people got to witness, yet not understand, the reality of Black people. All they could see was some object

---

[30] Carla Boos and Mirjam Gulmans, De Slavernij: Mensenhandel van de Koloniale Tijd Tot Nu (Amsterdam: Uitgeverij Balans, 2011).

[31] Ibid.

that, according to them, was equal to animals and not human beings. The color of their skin tone was different from that of the Whites. In their eyes, Blacks were inferior, and Whites were superior.

However, as I mentioned earlier, in contrast, what we know about the Black race is that Black people are not inferior to White people. According to anatomist Camper, the Black person does not differ from the White person. Under their skin, they have the same cells, they have the same red blood, and they have the same brain. Clearly, they possess the same functionality at every level of life.[32] It is interesting to see that history showed us that one of the main reasons the Europeans went to Africa was to get Black men who were strong, telling us that the strength of Black men was a significant trait. They were captured and taken to work in plantations as slaves, and because of their forced hard labor, they began to run the plantations for the Europeans. Black men were smart and innovative. They discovered a medicine that healed the Europeans.[33] They were also skilled workers on the plantation. They used their intelligence to flee the plantation and establish themselves in the jungle. These men had the know-how to be builders and the wisdom to keep some of their secrets from the Whites. They even have a song, until this day, in Suriname entitled, "Taantiri A No Dong," that says that quietness is not ignorance, meaning just because I am quiet does not mean I'm dumb; it just means that I don't want to reveal anything.

---

[32] Petrus Camper, "Petrus Camper on the Origin and Color of Blacks," n.d.

[33] Londa Schiebinger, Secret Cures of Slaves: People, Plants, and Medicine in the Eighteenth-Century Atlantic World (Standford: Stanford University Press, 2017). Londa L. Schiebinger, *Secret Cures of Slaves: People, Plants, and Medicine in the Eighteenth-Century Atlantic World* (Stanford, CA: Stanford University Press, 2017).

Figure 15 The Black Woman is Elegant and Beautiful

For women, history has also proven that Black women are the most beautiful women you can ever find. The Black woman has the resourcefulness to transform ashes into diamonds, a chameleon ability to conform to any environment effortlessly and shine, and a unique blend of sass, intellect, beauty, spirituality, warmth, and support that makes her irresistible to many. Black women are elegant and beautiful.

If we bring this same contrast into the 21st century, Black men today are world changers, great trendsetters, CEOs that help change the global spectrum, and leaders of the free world. They are not only leaders of the free world, but both Black men and women today are billionaires, great intellectuals, and scholars, and highly sought after for their leadership skills, creativity, strength, and problem-solving capabilities. They are also leading the way in athleticism, art, music, and cinematography.

Despite the stigmatism of inferiority that was historically ingrained within Black men and women, today they are determined to, more than ever, reach the top and cast down the lie that was told about them, and succeed no matter what. There is no turning back.

The Hypocrisy of Interracial Relationships

Interracial relationships are the relationships that break the barriers of curiosity when one steps out of his or her own race to have a romantic relationship with someone of another race. According to Van Vogenbrock's assault on Black men and women, you would think he and other leaders from the West India Company, such as Willem Bosman, would stay far away from Black women and would have nothing to do with them sexually. In contrast, these same men had Black women as servants working for them and, on many occasions, sexually assaulted the women, had relationships with them, and even impregnated them. Today, you will find Black people in Ghana with the last name "Bosman," who are descendants of the same Willem Bosman.[34] On one end, you see the hypocritic assault and stereotyping of Black men and women, but on the other hand, the same Black people being insulted are the ones being used for selfish ambition and gain.

---

[34] Carla Boos, *De Slavernij. Mensenhandel Van De Koloniale Tijd Tot Nu* (Amsterdam: Balans, 2011).

CHAPTER 3

THE PEOPLE OF NDYUKA

MALÓGASSI

"Di wi waka tee nee wi kai na Mama Ndyuka"

(After walking a long while, we arrived at Mother Ndyuka)

A n estimated 20% of Suriname's population are Maroons. They are known as runaway slaves that used to live on plantations. As a result, the African culture strongly influences the culture of the Maroons because of the people's African heritage. The Maroon culture is firmly rooted in West and Central African cultural traditions, with some Amerindian influences. In this chapter, as a Ndyuka, I will explain, in detail, some of my Ndyuka culture and tradition that can be traced back to West Africa, Ghana.

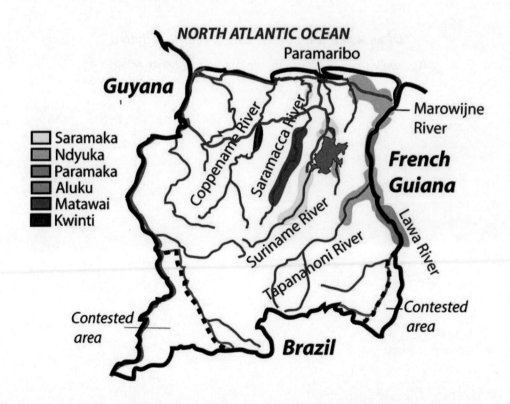

Figure 16 Map of Suriname Showing Areas Where the Maroons Are Settled

Overview

In Suriname, you are likely to find different groups of Maroons located across the country. Their occupancy even extends to French Guiana. The Ndyuka is the largest ethnic group of Maroons that live in Suriname, and their presence is concentrated around the Marowijne River.[35]

The Ndyuka culture, beliefs, and other practices are like other Maroon groups but still exhibit slight differences, making them unique. The Ndyuka people look similar to West Africans as it relates to their physical appearance. This is strongly influenced by the tradition of Ndyuka women and men only marrying within their Maroon community, causing them to remain genetically close to their African ancestors. This tradition has, however, changed in recent years as younger generations are more inclined to marry outside of their race.

Figure 17 Strong Ndyuka Warriors Who Gave the Colonial Soldiers a Run for their Money.

---

[35] "Ndyuka Collection," Milwaukee Public Museum, accessed March 23, 2022, https://www.mpm.edu/research-collections/anthropology/online-collections-research/ndyuka/mpm-collection.

The Language

Language is necessary for communication purposes. Every language follows a certain set of rules that determine how we sound when we are talking. The Ndyuka Maroons from Suriname are no exception to this rule. They use oral language that is named after them to communicate.

Ndyuka, which is also referred to as Aukan or Eastern Maroon Creole, or *Nenge,* is a form of creole language spoken in Suriname by the Ndyuka Maroons. Those Maroons were formerly called "Bush Negroes" and are also closely linked to the Maroons in French Guiana. Most of the Maroons who speak this language reside in the country's interior among the tropical rainforests. There are approximately 34,000 native speakers of the Ndyuka language up to the year 2011.[36] The language that they speak is classified under what is called English creole. They also have a form of dialect that is called Aluku. What exactly is the term "creole" and "dialect"?

According to the Collins dictionary, the term creole is "a language that has developed from a mixture of different languages and has become the main language in a particular place."[37] This, therefore, denotes that the Ndyuka creole is a mixture of languages to which they have been exposed and adapted, to create one main language. A dialect, on the other hand, according to the Cambridge dictionary, is "a form of language that people speak in a particular part of a country, containing some different words and grammar and pronunciations."[38]

The Ndyuka language, like any other language system, is made up of phonology and orthography. Phonology represents the sounds that are heard in

---

"Ndyuka," Ethnologue, accessed March 23, 2022, https://www.ethnologue.com/subgroups/suriname.

[37] "Definition of 'Creole,'" Collins Dictionary, last modified 2020, https://www.collinsdictionary.com/dictionary/english/creole.

[38] "Dialect," Cambridge Dictionary, last modified 2020, https://dictionary.cambridge.org/grammar/british-grammar/dialect.

a spoken language. These sounds follow set rules in most cases. Orthography is a set of conventions for how a language is written. This includes the norms of spelling, punctuation, and word breaks, among other conventions.

Phonology of the Language

The Ndyuka language is based on English words but has a mixture of African, Portuguese, and other languages, which influence the grammar and sounds of the words spoken. Britannica online states, "As much as 30% of the Ndyuka lexicon can be traced to English, 10% to Portuguese, and another 10% to Amerindian languages and Dutch. The grammar resembles that of the other, lexically distinct Atlantic Creoles and presumably derives from African models."[39] One example of how the mixture of the different languages influence the Ndyuka language, for instance, is the difference in tone between na ("is") and ná ("isn't"). Words can start with consonants such as mb and ng, and some speakers use the consonants kp and gb. An example of this is the word "to leave" which is gwé or gbé, from English "go away."

Orthography of the Language

In recent years, orthography differs from an older Dutch-based orthography in substituting "u" for "oe" and "y" for "j." Tone is a vital part of the language used to convey the specific meaning that is intended for the spoken words.

Dialects

There are three dialects associated with the Ndyuka language. These are proper Ndyuka (or Okanisi), Aluku, and Paramaccan. All three dialects are distinct

---

[39] "Ndyuka," Encyclopedia.Com, last modified 2021, https://www.encyclopedia.com/humanities/encyclopedias-almanacs-transcripts-and-maps/ndyuka.

based on ethnicity. Another language sometimes included among the Ndyuka group is Kwinti, although it is widely viewed as a separate language.

The Ndyuka people have a written language called the Afaka script. It consists of a syllabary of 56 letters devised in 1910. The script is named after its inventor, Afáka Atumisi, and is used to write Ndyuka. Afaka is the only script in use that was designed specifically for a creole or for a form of English. In this writing, there is only one punctuation mark called the pipe (|), which is equivalent to a comma or a full stop. Afaka initially used spaces between words, but not all writers have continued to do so. The origins of many of the letters are obscure, though they appear to be acrophonic rebuses, with many of these being symbols from Africa. Of note is the fact that the syllabary does not represent all the sounds of the Ndyuka language. Other notable features are that it is written from left to right, similar to English texts, and the letters are based on Latin and Arabic letters and numerals as well as African graphic symbols.

Example of the Written Language:
The Letters of the Alphabet in the English Creole

Figure 18 The Letters of the Alphabet in English Creole [40]

A Letter Written and Translated in the Ndyuka Language

---

[40] André RM Pakosie, CN Dubelaar, and Wim Hoogbergen, *Het Afakaschrift van de Tapanahoni in Suriname* (Amsterdam: Thela Thesis, 1999).

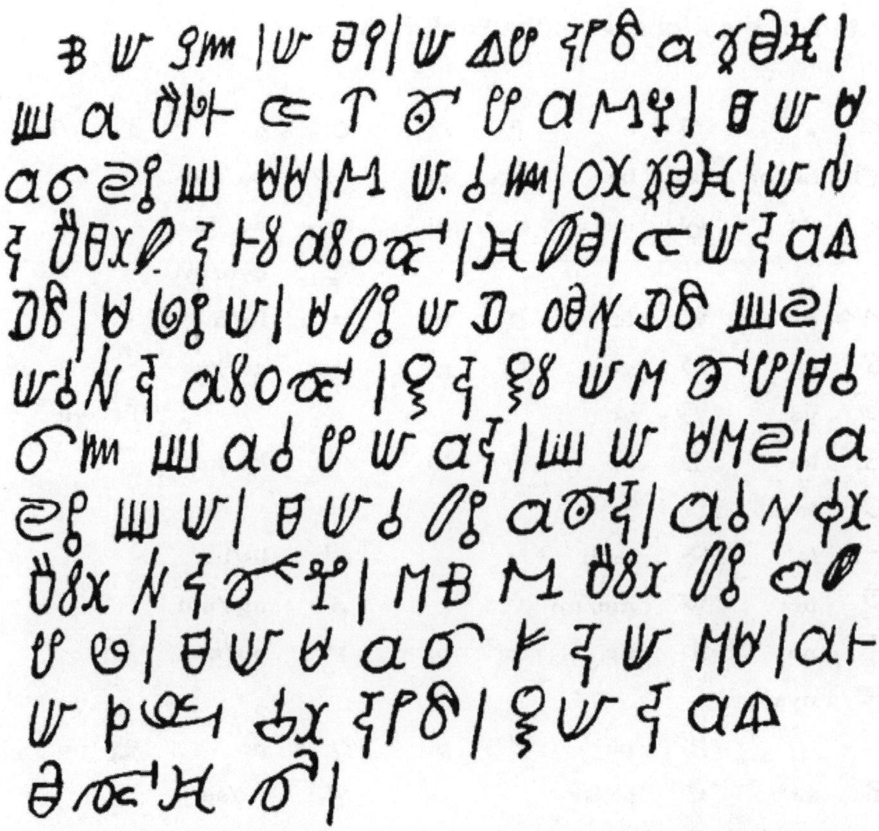

Figure 19 A Letter Written and Translated in the Ndyuka Language[41]

Text

ke mi gadu | mi masa | mi bigi na ini a kulotu |

fu a papila di yu be gi afaka | ma mi de

aga siki fu dede | fa mi sa du | oli kulotu | mi go

na pamalibo na lati ati oso | tu bolo | di mi ná abi

moni | de yaki mi | de taki mi mu oloko moni fosi |

mi sa go na ati osu | da na dati mi e begi | masa

---

[41] C.N. Dubelaar and J.W. Gonggryp, "De Geschriften Van Afaka in Zijn Djoeka-Schrift," *New West Indian Guide / Nieuwe West-Indische Gids* 42, no. 1 (January 1962): pp. 213-254, https://doi.org/10.1163/22134360-90002324.

gadu fu a sa gi mi ana | fu mi deesi | a

siki fu mi | ma mi sa taki abena | a sa kon tyali

patili go na ndyuka | eke fa patili taki a bun

gi wi | ma mi de aga pe na mi ede | ala

mi noso poli na ini ye | da mi ná abi

losutu ye |

Translation in English

Oh my God, my Lord, I start with the words on the paper you've given Afaka. But I'm deathly ill. How can I say it? I went to Paramaribo Lands Hospital two times. Because I have no money, they chased me away. They say I must first earn money (before) I go to the hospital. Therefore, I pray to the Lord God that he will give me a hand with the medicine for my illness. But I will talk to Abena. He will bring this to the Priest of the Ndyuka. So as the father says, it is good for us. But I have pain in my head. All my nose is rotting from the inside, I tell you. So, I have no rest, I tell you.

Text

En so den be abaa na a líba, dísi wi kai Kawína Líba. Di den abaa de, den abaa teke gwe na opu fu Kawína. En so den be waka langa langa gwe te na Mama Ndyuka ede, pe wi kai Mama Ndyuka.

Translation in English

And so, they crossed the river, which we call "Kawina [Commewijne] River." Having crossed it, they went way upstream along the Commewijne. Thus, they traveled a long, long way, clear to the upper Tapanahony, the place we call "Mama Ndyuka."

Spirituality

The term spirituality denotes the practice of being concerned with the human spirit or soul instead of material or physical things. The Ndyuka have numerous religious beliefs. They are adamant that the knowledge humans have is extremely limited, and therefore they believe that there are alternative paths to the unknown, which they highly treasure. They claim that many unknown things belong to the realm of the gods, of which they worship many different gods (gadu). They believe that these gods are powerful and immortal beings. In their opinion, these gods can live forever, and some are revered as omniscient, that is, knowing everything or omnipresent, the act of being present in every location at the same time.

The Ndyuka structure of deities has a three-tiered hierarchy. The god Masaa Gadu, known as the Lord God, occupies the peak of the supernatural hierarchy. The people view him as the "source of creation." Next, in the hierarchy below, Masaa Gadu is Gaan Gadu, also termed the Great Deity. Gaan Gadu is also known as Gaan Tata. He is viewed as the Great Father. There is also Gedeonsu, the God of Danger, to name a few from the third tier, below the top two. Based on their idea of the roles of their gods, they say that each of these deities "intervenes directly in human affairs, takes sides in conflicts, and punishes humans for their sins."[42]

Masaa Gadu

The unique roles of the deities are separated by the assumption that Masaa Gadu offers protection to everyone on equal levels; however, the other Great Deities are "tribal or national gods." The Ndyuka Maroons believe that Gaan Tata was extremely upset about the injustice that the Ndyuka suffered, and because of this, he emancipated them from slavery. Gaan Tata is believed to be a protector of

---

[42] Carole Boyce Davies, *Encyclopedia of the African Diaspora : Origins, Experiences, and Culture* (ABC-CLIO, 2008).

42

the Ndyuka people, shielding them from enemies, especially witches. This god is said to defend the Ndyuka cultural traditions, ensuring that certain things that are viewed as taboo remain as such and punish those who act as thieves, adulterers, and/or gays.

Ogii

Viewed as the king of the forest spirits, it is said that the people must appease this god because he possesses a tremendously destructive force.

Some Other Gods

Gedeonsu is said to shield the nation and provide comfort to the people and hear their prayers. They believe that he provides in times of hunger and famine and that he is faithful and always takes care of them if they remain faithful to him.[43]

Although multiple gods occupy the third tier, the Ndyuka people recognize four main ones. They are the yooka - Ancestor god, papa gadu or vodu - Reptile Spirits god, ampuku - Bush Spirits god, and kumanti - spirits that live in things like thunder, lightning, carrion birds, and other animals of prey.

It is interesting to note that the Ndyuka Maroons believe that many of their gods act like human beings where they "mate, procreate, and reproduce." They exhibit significant differences in their possession and use of the supernatural powers they're believed to possess. It is widely viewed by the Ndyuka that the deity's relationship with humans is either one of two extremes. They are either benevolent or hostile. Except for kumanti spirits, the deities can transform into hostile avenging spirits when they become offended.

---

[43] Thoden van Velzen, H. U. E., W. van Wetering, and Elst Dirk van der, *In the Shadow of the Oracle: Religion as Politics in a Suriname Maroon Society* (Long Grove, IL: Waveland Press, 2004).

Organized Worship

There is no known organized group that follows Masaa Gadu; however, the Great Deities Gaan Tata, Ogii, and Gedeonsu have organized groups of people who worship them. Shrines are dedicated to these gods with priests who lead worship in their places of worship. The organized groups that follow each of these deities are led by individuals called *obeah* (obia) man or "medicine men." Their religious system has persons who they proclaim to be prophets, some of whom have spiritual influence.

Religious practices greatly influence different ceremonies of the Ndyuka people. They hold that almost all spirits reveal themselves each year on New Year's Day. There are also Santi witchcraft rituals practiced by the followers of Gaan Tata. These rituals take place regularly, although they do not have fixed dates. Other rituals include those that claim to advance the well-being of all Ndyuka. These are observed every two or three years and are officiated by Gedeonsu's priests.

Figure 20 Image of Ceremonies by the Ndyuka Maroons

Of note is the assertion that minor deities act as spirit mediums for the greater deities to add more luster to their worship. When there are special occasions, for example, New Year's Day, or a fellow medium has died, they gather to do their religious dances under the supervision of respected medicine men called basi. These medicine men are said to be highly knowledgeable about the spirits that are being honored at these ceremonies.

There is a flagpole in the Ndyuka village which is considered to be the main shrine to the ancestors. The elders of the village gather here daily. They do this because they feel that the dead ancestors are constantly present among the living. So, at this shrine, they converse with these ancestors. They use the opportunity to intercede before the dead ancestors for liberation from sickness and bad fortune.

Example of a Ndyuka Shrine

Figure 21 Ndyuka Wooden Shrine

When there is a death among the Ndyuka people, there are prolonged rituals for up to a year or longer. These ceremonies are supervised by an association of gravediggers. This association includes coffin makers and other burial associations. The concept behind these drawn-out rituals is to ensure that the dead person's ghost reveals its secrets, which may be useful to those who are living. The dead bodies are viewed as sacred and worshipped. Those who claim to cross-examine the corpse do so to evaluate whether the person is removed from the village at once and is deemed as an upright person or a sinner. Those classified as sinners are taken to a site in the forest designated for such ones and buried in a shallow grave without a coffin. Those that are viewed as witches are left unburied as a sign of humiliation. In general, they believe that witches and sinners are killed by god and should not be esteemed with an elaborate funeral. However, those that are gracious are honored with an esteemed and elaborate funeral.

Traditional Marriage

Traditionally, marriage among the Ndyuka people is exogamous, meaning marriage outside of one's social group. In the Ndyuka society, marriages within the same lineage have become widely accepted; however, marriage to two sisters is not permitted. The Ndyuka Maroons view this as incestuous, which is taboo and frowned upon. Marriage and sexual intercourse with a wife's sister are two of the greatest sins that they believe will arouse the wrath of the ancestors.

It is estimated that among the Ndyuka Maroons, almost one-third of marriages are polygynous, which means having multiple wives. This is only done if the man can afford to maintain more than one household. Divorce is allowed and is common and easy to obtain. Marriage with this Maroon group is viewed as a contractual agreement between individuals and kin groups. Unlike other societies where it is a one-time arrangement that ends only at the death of a spouse or with divorce, in the Ndyuka culture, it is a continuous bargaining process. The marriage arrangement shapes their social organizations as well as their customs. Although it is socially acceptable in the Ndyuka tradition for a man to have multiple wives (but it does not usually exceed three), as well as lovers or potential wives, he must ensure that he provides for his wives and maintains their affections. The husband must give his wives a house, a garden plot, a canoe and paddle, a hammock and mosquito net, and various household utensils. He also does this by hunting and fishing for her, clearing gardens in the forest, and building houses and canoes. The wives reciprocate by giving their own clothing gifts such as breechcloths, capes, shirts, and handkerchiefs.

The marriage ceremony consists of a formal meeting of the woman's matriclan resulting in a verbal contract by the man. The man requests permission from the woman's parents, and upon consent, the marriage takes place. The contract is signed by the woman agreeing to give birth to the man's children and the man agreeing to provide materially for his wife. Their marriage is a verbal contract.

Figure 22 Ndyuka Couple

When two persons are newlyweds, they may live in the village where the wife originated. They sometimes agree to live interchangeably in both the man's village and the woman's village. In later years, they may decide to live permanently in the man's village, especially if he has risen to the rank of the headman in the village. Many people in the Ndyuka community have houses in more than one village. House ownership is an individual matter. Upon marriage, a man will build a house for his wife in her village and cut her garden plot, whether he intends to settle there or not. He will also maintain a house in his lineage's village. It is not unusual for a man to own a third house in his father's village. Because nearly one out of every three men has more than one wife, the number of houses and garden plots that must be kept in a good state may rise above three. The woman's role in the family after marriage is diverse. They are responsible for growing food, cooking, sewing clothes, and making cookware. The children reside with their mother for the first few years of life, and then a male child may be given to a father or uncle to be raised into adulthood. The men are responsible for fishing and hunting, making houses and canoes, and felling trees in forest areas being cleared for gardens. They also spend time on the coast sometimes, working to earn money to purchase necessary goods such as cloth and tools.

Example of the Woman and Man's role:

Figure 23 Ndyuka Woman Cooking

Figure 24 Dugout Canoe

Divorce

To obtain a divorce, the man informs his wife's matriclan's leaders that he no longer wants to be her husband. If the man has wronged the woman in some way, a fine is levied by the matriclan to appease the ancestral spirits. It is said that if a woman "overpowers" a man by her attitudes and actions, that man should divorce his wife and go back to his own village. People, especially men, must travel a lot. In the Tapanahony River area, if one excludes the 15% of all marriages that are autolocal, in which partners pay only brief visits to each other, about a third of all adults live polylocally, with more than one place of residence. For a man, this implies that he cannot identify too closely with one domestic unit since this would mean a loss of maneuverability in other groups. It is imperative to spread his interests over several villages, depending on how many wives he has.

Traditional Attire and Community Goods

Style of dress forms an integral part of every culture. This aspect of culture is one identifying mark of specific groups of people. The Ndyuka people have a unique style of dress. Often, the woman goes topless or wears a bra only. A woman in the Ndyuka culture wears clothing that consists of what is called a pangi that is worn to her waist and a cloth tied across her right shoulder. You would see her upper thigh, buttocks, and pelvic area always covered with a pangi – a one-piece wrap-around cloth. She also wears several rings above her ankles. Sometimes, men wear a mixture of traditional dress and Western dress (especially hats) to formal occasions. The men often go topless or wear the kamisa (a toga-like cloth thrown over one shoulder and caught with a knot).

Another feature of their adornment is decorative scarring called cicatrization. Women usually do this, and these designs are viewed as important parts of beauty and sexuality. Women get their cicatrization redone every few months and gradually reduce the frequency over the years. This leads to the scar becoming permanent over time. At that point, they do not have to do it again. The women take a long time to comb and braid their hair. They wear a variety of accessories that add to their adornment. These include calf bands, anklets, earrings, necklaces, and armbands. Ndyuka women usually stack aluminum anklets to shape the lower leg into a cylindrical shape.

Figure 25 Example of the Ndyuka Style of Dress, Hair combing, Scars, and Jewelry

Figure 26 Braided Hair

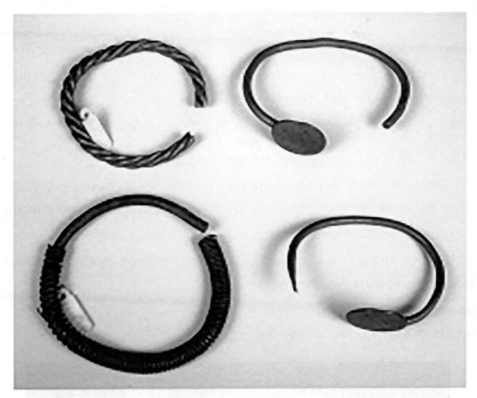

Figure 27 Metal Armbands

Goods Found in the Community

The main economic activity in the Ndyuka community is agriculture. They grow crops for their personal use as well as for a small group of related family members. The main crop they produce is dry rice. Other crops include cassava, taro, okra, maize, plantains, bananas, sugar cane, and peanuts. They also hunt and fish, which contributes significantly to their economy. They do not have markets; their catches are shared among their kinsmen.

Items are purchased from external communities. They are then brought into the village. These commodities include shotguns, tools, pots, cloth, hammocks, beds, salt, soap, kerosene, rum, outboard motors, cars, electronics, televisions, transistor radios, and stereo systems.

Art

The Ndyuka people are producers of different types of artworks. Men are usually considered the masters of creating artwork. They make wood carvings that are usually very stylish and elaborate. These include boat oars, trays, canoes, and houses. They regularly paint the doors of their homes in very bright colors, as well as their boat oars.

Women, on the other hand, downplay their artistic abilities. They carve out calabash bowls, ladles, and containers. Women also sew and cross-stitch designs on their husbands' kamisa (a toga-type garment thrown over one shoulder and caught with a knot). Giving artistic gifts that have been carefully made is an important expression of love between spouses.

Examples of Some Goods Produced

Figure 28 Carved out Calabash Bowls, Spoons, and Dishes

The Ndyuka people are widely recognized for woodcarving art. It is said that men usually use this to express love and affection. Because their tradition is for men and women to give gifts to maintain their relationship, the creation of these commodities is not taken lightly. Carved items include beautiful wooden objects made in the form of utilitarian objects, such as food stirrers, combs, trays, paddles, and clothes.

Food Stirrer

Figure 29 Food Stirrer

Clothes Beater

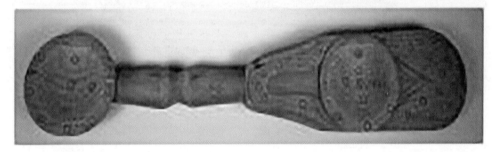

Figure 30 Clothes Beater

It is noteworthy that the most valuable commodity women cherish in the Ndyuka culture is combs. This is because combs are one of the most magnificent pieces in their craftsmanship, and women also use them in styling and ornamenting their hair. They serve as personal objects that women treasure and display as symbols of wealth.

Examples of Comb

Figure 31 Combs

Peanut Grinding Boards

Figure 32 Peanut Grinding Boards

Stools

It is taboo in Ndyuka culture for a person to sit on the ground, so these are essential commodities that are often carried around for use.

Figure 33 Stool Adorned with Women Making Fufu by Pounding Cassava and Yams

Music and Drums
Drums

Drums play a key role in both the Ndyuka artistic and religious traditions. The Ndyuka believe that drums are important in communicating with the gods. They are used in worship along with singing and dancing. The drums are made from wood and animal skin. In the Ndyuka culture, the traditional apinti drum is a round, compact instrument made of cedarwood and goatskin, designed to be played while sitting. The apinti drum is traditionally upright and is sometimes substituted with congas. The apinti drum is a "talking drum" used at major council meetings and certain important rituals.

Figure 34 Example of the Apinti Drum

Playing Aleke Music

Figure 35 Playing Aleke Music

The Ndyuka Maroons have their own unique styles of musical culture. The music is different from that of Africa but has some African elements to it. Aleke is the most common music among them. Every Ndyuka dance has its own rhythm and hand clap associated with it. Drums are used for various reasons, such as secular dance forms, making announcements within the village, supervising, and commenting on proceedings at council meetings, and rituals designed to communicate with the spirits.

Dance styles include, but are not limited to Mato, Susa, Songe, Awasa, Aleke, and Tuka. The only dance that is not accompanied by music and the rattling of the ankle chains is the Mato. Mato is a dance that is associated with a folktale. A folktale is a story originating in popular culture, typically passed down by word of mouth. A synonym for Mato is Anansi toli, or, simply put, Anansi stories. Many, but not all, of these Matos, revolve around the mythical spider known as Anansi, a West African trickster figure that originated with the Akan-speaking people of Ghana. These stories in their culture are usually told during periods following a death. The term mato also refers to an entire genre of music and dance associated with formal funerary rites. During these dances, stories are not usually told in their entirety, but instead, different performers compete for attention, jumping out suddenly and launching into a new tale, often interrupting the one that came before. The stories serve as a pretext for the performance of the songs associated with them.

Performing a Mato

Figure 36 Dancers Show their Dancing Skills

Susa resembles a western world dance show where dancers show their dancing skills. There is drumming with vocals, and two male dancers display their dancing skills. This dance is like a game. It includes two male dancers facing each other, and they have to anticipate each other's moves. The spectators who surround the dancers cheer them on by singing and clapping as well as gesturing and cheering.

Figure 37 Playing Songe Music

Songe can be referred to as both dancing and drumming. During the songe, women dance by imitating a fish defending its fry, while the men act as fishermen with arrows and bows. Songe music, when performed for dancing, is based on a combination of three wooden drums. These are the gaan doon, a large drum that serves as the lead instrument, the pikin doon, a small drum that plays a supporting role, and the atompai, which is played with a stick and one hand. These drums vary only slightly in size. A percussion instrument, known as the kwakwa, is also an important part of this musical performance.

Figure 38 Ndyuka Dancing Awasa in Traditional Attire. Awasa Allows a Woman to Show Off Her Beauty and a Man to Display his Dancing Skills. Aleke Songs are About Social Events that Occur in Everyday Village Life.

Tuku is performed during mourning rituals. This includes lamentation songs that are done before the funeral of a deceased person. The dancers, one in front of the other, form a tight ring and shuffle slowly around the body. This music uses a single drum.

Food

> *"A koni fu den gaansama fu wi, meki wi a taan anga angii"*
> *(The knowledge of our ancestors caused us not to go hungry)*

Food is always referred to as the staff of life. It is rightly called one of human's basic needs because our days on this earth are short-lived without it. Every culture has different types of food its people consume. The Ndyuka people have foods that may not be unique to them, but we will still explore some of them. The Ndyuka menu consists of farm items and things that they acquire from hunting and fishing. The major garden crop they consume is dry rice. Other crops include cassava, taro, okra, maize, plantains, bananas, sugarcane, and peanuts. They also have as part of their diet, coconut, orange, breadfruit, and papaya.

Figure 39 Rice Ready for Harvest

Rice is the seed of a kind of grass species. It is a cereal grain that the Ndyuka people consume. This staple food is the main item on their dietary list.

Ndyuka Women Cooking

Figure 40 Ndyuka Woman Making Cassava Bread

Taro

This is a root tuber that grows underground. Another name for taro is eddo or dasheen. This starchy food is cooked and eaten as a staple by the Ndyuka Maroons. This staple is their primary source of carbohydrates.

Taro or Dasheen being grown

Figure 41 Taro or Dasheen Tuber, which is Eaten by the Ndyuka Maroons

Cassava

This is also a root tuber which is a staple food of the Ndyuka people. While they may consume cassava cooked in various manners, it should not be eaten raw, as this is deadly. Common commodities such as flour and bread are derived from cassava. It can also be used to make other things such as puddings and cakes. Along with rice, this is another primary source of carbohydrates.

What the Cassava Looks Like

Figure 42 Cassava Root

Figure 43 Cassava Bread

Maize

A common name for maize is corn, and it is a cereal grain. This food is cooked by either boiling or by grinding it into other products such as flour. It can also be roasted. Their consumption of corn provides rich sources of fiber, vitamins, and minerals, as well as carbohydrates.

Corn on the Cob

Figure 44 Corn

Plantains and Bananas

Plantains are sometimes confused with bananas which are smaller in size. Plantains can be eaten green when cooked using a variety of cooking methods or can be eaten ripe. When consumed green, it is a source of carbohydrates, and when eaten ripe, it is a good source of vitamins and minerals

Figure 45 Green Plantain and Ripe Plantain

Figure 46 Green Bananas and Ripe Bananas

Sugarcane

This is a grass that the Ndyuka people grow. It is cultivated for its juice which is sweet. It can be eaten immediately after reaping or can be processed to get other products such as sugar, rum, or other alcoholic products.

Figure 47 Sugarcane Crop

Other Produce - Peanuts

Figure 48 Peanuts

Okra

Figure 49 Okra

Fishing and Hunting

One of the things that they hunt is wild pigs. They also catch fish using the canoes that they construct.

Figure 50 Wild Pigs

CHAPTER 4

I AM OKANSI:
DISCOVERING SELF IN HISTORY
AND SHARED STORIES

MALOGASSI

"Wadaa!" (from *"Werda?"* (Who's there?)) to which the guest was expected to reply: *"Fiiman"* (a free man).

I am an Okanisi man. The Okanisi or Ndyuka are one of the largest Maroon tribes. We, the Okanisi, call ourselves Maroons but not like the runaway beast in the dictionary of the western world, nor as identified in the Dutch or English dictionary. When the Okanisi call themselves Maroons, it is a proclamation that we are descendants of self-emancipators. I come from a generation of people who know how to network to gain their freedom. I descend from people who know how to strategically navigate and spread intelligence to liberty. My ancestors know their historical identity and recognize their value – people who exude self-worth. That is why we call ourselves Maroons.

Slaves entered Suriname under the harshest of conditions.[44] It was the worst type of slavery in the world, as I have been told. The atrocities against humanity were most prevalent during the years of slavery. People were killed in the most unbelievable ways. Thrown into scorching water heated to a maximum temperature for processing sugar. The big pot used to cook sugarcane juice, known as the Kappa, can still be found at Fort Zeelandia today, along with remnants of the site where they would burn slaves to death in excruciating water.

---

[44] Gert Oostindie, "Voltaire, Stedman and Suriname Slavery," *Slavery & Abolition* 14, no. 2 (1993): pp. 1-34, https://doi.org/10.1080/01440399308575095.

Figure 51 Kappa in Front of Fort Zeelandia

When slaves attempted to escape, slave masters would hang the attempted escapees by their ribcage using a sharp hook. This ensured the slaves died in slow agony as they took their time dismembering their body parts, beginning with an arm, and leg, and finally slaughtering them.

There was a lot of brutality taking place in Suriname. Slave masters would cut the breasts of young, beautiful slave women and kill them in that manner – as they bled to death.[45] Additionally, they would kill babies by drowning them in the Suriname River next to Fort Zeelandia. When a baby was crying, you had women that would take the baby, submerge them into the river and drown them. After drowning the baby, they would pull the baby out, give them back to the mother and say, "I've silenced your baby." This is just one of many stories that would send chills down anyone's spine.

---

[45] Jenny Sharpe, *Ghosts of Slavery: A Literary Archaeology of Black Women's Lives* (Minneapolis, MN: Univ. of Minnesota Press, 2003).

Maria Susanna Duplessis

Susanna du Plessis or Maria Susanna Duplessis lived in a beautiful and historic building still located right across from the presidential palace in Paramaribo. Mrs. Duplessis was a very wealthy and well-connected woman. She was influential and played an essential role in decision-making on some of the plantations. One day, her husband was said to be flirting with one of his maids when his wife walked in on them. Under normal circumstances, she would be furious and let her voice be heard, but she kept silent. During dinnertime, she invited her husband to come to the dinner table. When her husband lifted the cloche over his plate, he saw the breast of the maid. That was just one of the many horrible things she did to the Africans. Mrs. Duplessis was known in the city for killing the babies of African women. She was one of several who drowned crying babies. When babies would cry, she approached the mother politely and asked them if she could help them soothe the baby. Of course, if someone of her stature asks you to hand your baby over to help you, you do so. The mother would hand over their baby to Mrs. Duplessis and Mrs. Duplessis would take the baby to paata booki (flat

Figure 52 Maria Susanna Duplessis

bridge) on the Suriname River and hold the baby upside down by its feet with its head submerged in the water until they drowned. She would then bundle the baby back in their blankets, bring them back to their mothers, and tell them, "I've silenced the baby for you. They are no longer crying." These are some of the atrocities African women had to endure at the hand of Mrs. Duplessis.

Where We Came From

- In Suriname, they shipped in approximately 550,000 slaves from Africa between 1651 and 1800 from four primary regions: The Windward Coast, the Slave Coast, the Gold Coast, and the Loango.[46] The western colonizers went to Africa to get strong Africans, but the focus was primarily on these regions where enslaved Africans came from:

    - Upper Guinea Coast: The area outlined by the Senegal and Gambia Rivers

    - Ivory (or Kwa Kwa or Windward) Coast: Central Liberia

    - Lower Guinea Coast: Divided into the Gold Coast on the west (Cote d'Ivoire and Ghana), the Slave Coast (Togo, Benin, and western Nigeria), and the Bight of Benin (Nigeria and Cameroon)

    - Gabon

    - Angola

Due to the varied cultural influences, distinctive dialects were formed, such as the Sranantongo and Okanisi tongo (the language of the Okanisi). When slavery was abolished, there were only 22,000 people of African descent still alive. These 22,000 Africans ensured that emancipation took place. The emancipation did not

---

[46] Gary Brana-Shute and Wim Hoogbergen, "The History of the Suriname Maroons," in *Resistance and Rebellion in Suriname: Old and New* (Williamsburg: Dept. of Anthropology, College of William and Mary, 1990), pp. 65-102.

happen because they wanted it to happen, or because some Europeans were protesting it, it happened because Whites were forced to abolish slavery. Yes, White Christians were protesting the slave trade and slavery in the Western hemisphere, but emancipation happened because of the Maroons. They emancipated themselves from this harsh form of slavery in Suriname. From the late 1670s, the continuous expansion of the plantation economy led to an increasing number of African slave imports, and consequently, attacks by the Amerindians.

The battle that took place was known as the War of Indians (1668-1685).[47] This war caused plantations to cease expansion across the Suriname river and began to be rerouted eastward. The growth of the slave population began to decline as a result. Almost from their moment of arrival, slaves began to run away, although this increased substantially after the War of Indians. They went to the remote places to live – across waterfalls and mountains. Many went and established themselves, but they would not stay there. Maroons would come back and attack and raid the plantation. The colonialists continuously staged attacks against the Maroons, sending military patrols into the jungle to seize or kill them and to destroy their villages and provision grounds. In retaliation, while waging war against the plantation owners, Maroons came in and rescued their brothers and sisters, stealing resources such as hardware, rifles, and gunpowder, and kidnapping women to take as wives. During this period in Suriname, whenever they would come to get their brothers and sisters, they would have an intelligence network to support them among the slaves in Paramaribo.[48]

Some of them, I have been told, did not see a single plantation. Instead, immediately upon their arrival by ship, they had their brothers, like agents, among

---

[47] Van der Linden, Marcel. "The Okanisi: A Surinamese Maroon Community, C.1712–2010," *International Review of Social History* 60, no. 3 (September 2015): pp. 463-490, https://doi.org/10.1017/s0020859015000383.

[48] David Jamison, "From Resistance to Marronage: Slave Networks and the Forging of Identity in the Dutch Guianas, 1763--1823" (dissertation, ProQuest Dissertations Publishing, 2014), pp. 1-24.

the people giving them instructions on how to escape, and they would support them in running away to their freedom. From the generational stories that have been passed down to me outlining the oral history of Suriname, people of African descent, namely self-emancipators, would leave the ships and seek freedom in the forests of Suriname.[49] The Suriname forest looked like the African forest from where they originated. They knew the trees; they knew the plants, so they could take care of themselves. I heard a story; even children born prematurely could live in what was called the interior, an open space that contained Maroon and Amerindian villages and surrounding agricultural remnants without needing the confines of a hospital. Mothers knew how to keep the baby warm, safe, serene, and clean because the women knew how to do it. My grandmother, Ma Wasai, a tall, beautiful woman with long, natural hair, had only a first-grade education, and she served as one of the village's midwives.

Similar to when the Jews fled from Egypt, the Africans received manna from God. These self-emancipated African people, for example, would plant a plantain tree in the morning, and in the evening time, they would eat plantain from the harvest. It was quite a miracle to witness. The Africans possessed the knowledge, indigenous to their people, of how to grow plantains, how to cultivate them, and how to process them for consumption. The majority of these runaway Africans would not die of hunger, nor did they have to go back to the plantation to get food because they were self-sufficient in cultivating their own food. Stories have been told about how they had a network with the Amerindian Indians, who were the indigenous people of Suriname. The Amerindians would provide the Africans with cassava and a lot of seeds to plant.

---

[49] Junius P. Rodriguez, *Encyclopedia of Emancipation and Abolition in the Transatlantic World* (Armonk, NY: M.E. Sharpe, 2007).

Figure 53 The Provision Ground

The farming process originating from the Amerindians included strategic cultivation. Men would clear and set ablaze a section of the woods during drought season. Several days after the fire, women would begin to plant the provision grounds. After the soil became exhausted of its nutrients, they would then leave and go plant on new grounds.[50] After a decade or more, they would return and clear away the bush "kawee" and begin again. In addition to the cassava, there were basics like rice, yam, and banana also cultivated. These provision grounds were also misleading due to them being distanced from the villages, isolated and well-camouflaged. The practice of strategically hiding the provision grounds stemmed from slavery times as the ancestors fled to freedom.

---

[50] Londa L. Schiebinger, *Plants and Empire: Colonial Bioprospecting in the Atlantic World* (Cambridge, MA: Harvard University Press, 2007).

Figure 54 This is a Kawee

During this time, the Whites were constantly waging war against the Africans, and as such, the villages often had to be deserted without notice. While the Africans stayed prepared to relocate residence, their life source was derived from the provision ground, so the ground became a sacred place to preserve at all costs. Access was made challenging, and trail indicators were vague and misleading to ward off possible attacks. The Africans were intelligent enough to carry rice in their possession when they left Africa.

In 2006, a professor from UCLA led assistants and students into the interior of Suriname to look for the African type of rice they were growing in the Maroon communities.[51] During that visit, they found rice that was brought from Africa. The Africans knew food was fundamental, so they hid it in their hair during transport. They would braid their hair with rice carefully woven into their hair strands, making it unseen by the naked eye. One of the most popular women that brought rice from the plantation into the faraway forest of Suriname was Ma Pansa and her

---

[51] Judith A. Carney, *Black Rice: The African Origins of Rice Cultivation in the Americas* (Cambridge: Harvard University Press, 2009).

brother Chapana. Ma Pansa is the mother of one of the most prominent tribes, the Saamaka Tribe.

Scholars who came to Suriname wrote numerous stories about the Saramaka people. The spelling of the word, Saramaka, however, differs from the pronunciation. In speaking, one would say "*Saamaka*" as the correct pronunciation. During the early 1700s, many Maroon communities began to consolidate after fleeing slavery. The first massive community of runaways, formed in 1712, was attacked by French corsair, Jacques Cassard.[52] In an attempt to keep their human labor capital from being stolen, plantation owners temporarily sent their slaves into the woods to hide. Around 700 slaves decided to remain free, not returning to the plantation, and became the foundation of the Saamaka community, with their number expanding to the realm of 1,600 by the year 1749.

The next largest tribe in Suriname is the Okanisi or Ndyuka. Among the Okanisi are heroes, unknown to the land of Suriname but only depicted in oral history. What happened when those self-emancipated Africans went into the forest? They regrouped themselves in tribes with their unique hierarchy of tribalism as it exists in Africa.

The Maroon societies of Suriname are primarily based on the kinship of the mother or female line; men assume pivotal positions at the administrative and political levels. The political hierarchy of representatives is structured as:

- The Gaanman (King, Kondee masaa)

- The Ede Kabiten (Head Captain)

- The Kabiten (Captain or village headman)

- The Basia (Assistant)

---

[52] Karwan Fatah-Black, "White Lies and Black Markets: Evading Metropolitan Authority in Colonial Suriname, 1650-1800," *The Atlantic World* 31 (2015), https://doi.org/10.1163/9789004283350.

The leaders are chosen at tribal councils (*kuutu*) or meetings. The appointment and inauguration of these officials occur according to the Ndyuka tradition. After installation, each official officer, upon recommendation, is assigned and sworn in by the Surinamese government for purposes of receiving formal recognition and an official monthly salary.

The Gaanman

The Gaanman is the head chief of the Gaan lo of the Ndyuka, elected from the

Otoo-lo (Otoo clan). He is the leader with the most rights and represents the Ndyuka community. He is the headman of the board (*lanti*) and is considered sacred. The position and purpose of the Gaanman is the oldest of all the political organizations. All these leaders receive a monthly allowance from the government.

The Ede Kabiten

The Ede Kabiten represents the Gaanman, who is the supreme authority. The role of the Ede Kabiten is to oversee the administration of a specific region. He has been given the power to run one or multiple villages.

The Kabiten

The Kabiten is the most essential leader of the village, both socially and politically, and acts as public and external relations for the village. A Kabiten can have several assistants depending on the village population.

The Basia

The Basia are both male and female assistants. The male Basia assists the more esteemed officials in conducting ritual and administrative matters. The tasks of the female Basia are limited to domestic operations.

The Gaanman served as the governor of this group. All Gaanmans have aides, and just like in the army, everybody listens to them. The tribes then created clans. A community could have a tribe with 12 clans or more, but they speak most notably about the 12 primary clans. They call them the 12 Lo. Each lo established their own village or villages composed of dozens to up to hundreds of dwellings.[53] We have six of these tribes in Suriname: 1) Ndyuka, 2) Saamaka, 3) Matawai, 4) Pamaka, 5) Aluku, and 6) Kwinti.

Table 3.1 List of Gaanman or Kings and Their Lo (clan)

The Ndyuka Gaanman from 1759	The Saamaka Gaanman from 1762
Fabi Labi Beyman (Dikan-lo) 1759-1764	Abibi (Matyau-lo) 1762-1767
Kwamina Adyubi (Dikan-lo) 1764-1765	Kwaku Etya (Nasi-lo) 1775-1783
Abato Langaofangi Agaamu (Nyanfai-lo) 1765-1767	Alabi (Awana-lo) 1783-1820
Pamu Langabaiba (Otoo-lo) 1767-1790	Gbagidi Gbano (Matyau-lo) 1821 died in the same year
Toni (Otoo-lo, lebibee) 1790-1808	Kofi Gbosuma (Nasi-lo) 1822-1835
Bambi Kukudyaku Bonponubontanafe (Otoolo, baakabee) 1808-1819	Abaan Wetiwoyo (Matyau-lo) 1835-1867
Kwau Toobi (Otoo-lo, lebibee) 1820-1832	Faansi Bona (Awana-lo, Agbo-beu) 1870-1886
Pikin Pangaboko (a.i.) (Misidyan-lo) 1832-1833	Akoosu (Langu-lo) 1888-1897
	Moana Dyankusu (Matyau-lo) 1898-1932
	Binoutu Atudendu Antoni (Matyau-lo) 1934-1949

---

[53] Genia Julliette Lank Corinde, "Effective Collaboration between the Traditional Authority of the Maroon and the Central Government in Suriname: A Case Study at Resort Brownsweg" (University of Brasilia, 2017).

Manyan Beyman (Otoo-lo, baakabee) 1833-1866	Jozef Daniel Agbago Aboikoni (Matyau-lo) 1950-1989
Abaan Beeymofu (Otoo-lo, baakabee) 1867-1882	Songo-Aboikoni (Matyau-lo) 1991-2003
Oseyse (Otoo-lo, baakabee) 1884-1915	Belfon Aboikoni (Matyau-lo) 2005-2014
Yensa Kanape (a.i.) (Otoo-lo, baakabee) 1915-1916	Albert Aboikoni 2018-present
Papa Amakiti (Otoo-lo, baakabee) 1916-1929	
Yensa Kanape (a.i.) (Otoo-lo, baakabee) 1929-1937	
Pai Amatodya (Otoo-lo, baakabee) 1937-1947	
Apianai (a.i.) (Misidyan-lo, maasaabee) 1947-1950	
Akontu Velanti (Otoo-lo, baakabee) 1950-1964	
Adan Pankuku (a.i.) (Otoo-lo, lebibee) 1964-1966	
Gazon Sokoton Matodja (Otoolo, baakabee) 1966-2011	
Bono Velanti Otoo (Baaka bee) 2015 – Present	

The Matawai Gaanman from 1769	The Pamaka Gaanman from 1901
Dodo Musinga 1769-1778	Pertus Apensa (Antoosi-lo) 1901-1923
Beku 1778-1788	Jozef Abunawooko (Antoosi-lo) 1931-1947
Boyo 1788-1810	Cornelis Zacharias Forster (Antoosi-lo) 1950-1991
Koyo 1810-1830	
Afiti Yonkuman 1830-1853	
Josua Kaakun 1853-1867	

Faka Noah Adrai Vroomhart (was a Ndyuka) 1870-1893 Johannes King 1895-1896 Agubaka Lafanti 1898-1901 Mantili 1905-1908 Koso 1913-1918 Asaf Kine 1926-1947 Alfred Johan Abone Lafanti (Hanbei-lo) 1950-1980 Oscar Charles Lafanti (Hanbei-lo) 1981-2009 Lemsley Valentijn 2011-present	Atyode Markus Akilingi Kamili (a.i.) 1991-1993 Jan Levi (Antoose-lo) 1993-2008 Samuel Forster since 2010-2017 Jozef Misajere Forster 2020-present

The Kwinti Gaanman	The Aluku or Boni Gaanman
Boku Unknown-1765 Kofi Unknown-1827 Alamu 1887-Unknown. Officially appointed but not as Gaanman and only the tribe living on the Coppename River. Marcus Mentor 1913-1926 Paulua Paaka 1928-1936 Johannes Afiti 1937-1977 Matheus Cornelis Marcus 1978-1999 André Mathias 2002-2018. First to rule as Gaanman. Remon Clemens 2020-present	Askikan Silvester (Loamgu)....Unknown-1765 Oduamaa Kwadyo Kwadyani Aluku 1765-1792 Boni Kikindo (Loangu) 1765-1793 Agoso (Dikan-lo) 1793-1810 Gongo (Dikan-lo) 1812-1840 Obi Adan (Dikan-lo) 1842-1870 Atiaba (Yakobi-lo) 1872-1876 Anato (Yakobi-lo) 1876-1891 Osyi (Dikan-lo) 1893-1915 Awensai (Dikan-lo) 1917-1936 Difu (Dikan-lo) 1939-1967 Tolinga (Kawina-lo) 1969-1990 Paul Pakoti Doudou (Kawina-lo) 1992-2014. Residence in Papaïchton. Joachim-Joseph Adochini (Lape-lo) 1992 – present. Chosen by an election and not part of the maternal lineage. Residence in Maripasoula.

(Wetering and Thoden van Velzen, 2013)[54]

People in Suriname refer to the Okanisi as "Okan," but the name they call themselves is Okanisi or Ndyuka, the Okanisi Maroons in southeast Suriname. The word "Djuka," as written in many books and articles, is not the correct name. Djuka has a different connotation than Ndyuka. Both Ndyuka and Okanisi reflect a name of pride; Djuka, on the other hand, is a derogatory name. Thus, one would not want to be called Djuka. Unfortunately, as most people have trouble pronouncing Ndyuka correctly, they revert to saying Djuka, which is viewed as highly offensive to my tribe. This is mainly deemed as offensive because the river that they situated themselves on is called the Ndyuka River. Hence, they inherited the name of the Ndyuka people because they were living alongside the Ndyuka River.

This Ndyuka River has islands, both big and small in the landscape. These self-emancipators would go and make their village on these islands. No soldier of the colonialist army could come and get them because they did not know the safest way to reach these villages. The self-emancipators were the only ones that knew, as they were much more familiar with the challenging geographical terrain of the island landscape. Individuals would be afraid to go into the rapids, as they would be killed. As a result, the colonial leaders created their own Black army, known as the Black Rangers, to aid the troops in their struggle with the village populations.[55] The Black Rangers consisted of slaves purchased by the colonial government and shipped into dispatch on specified missions. The colonial leaders would have them trained as soldiers to go and capture these self-emancipators, or as they called them, Runaways and Maroons. While the Black Rangers were given provision grounds and received payment for each dispatch mission; however, some began to rebel, pillaging numerous plantations, killing some Whites, and then fleeing

---

[54] Velzen and Velzen, "Een Zwarte Vrijstaat in Suriname (Deel 2) – De Okaanse Samenleving in de Negentiende En Twintigste Eeuw."

[55] Rosemarijn Hoefte, "Free Blacks and Coloureds in Plantation Suriname," *Slavery & Abolition* 17, no. 1 (1996): pp. 102-129, https://doi.org/10.1080/01440399608575178.

inland once word spread that the Governor-General expected to diminish their prestige and living conditions.

Battles were ongoing between the colonial soldiers and the Maroons as they regularly attacked plantation colonies, robbing plantation owners of resources and women, claiming them for their own. Like other groups of Maroons, the Okanisi waged a constant war against the planters. Although colonial leaders attempted to counteract such terrorism with the enforcement of the Black Rangers, Maroon executions, and the destruction of village resources, they remained at an impasse. These constant bloody conflicts and the memory of the atrocities of slavery permeated the culture of the Okanisi and instilled in them a fundamental and persistent mistrust of White people.[56]

Until well into the 20th century, the sentry would greet those coming to visit the village with: "*Wadaa!*" (from Werda? Who's there?) to which the guest was expected to reply, "*Fiiman*" (a free man). *Wadaa* was a secret language or code that the Maroons in the plantation knew amongst each other. They knew that when they escaped to meet with their fellow escaped Maroons they would be greeted with the word, *Wadaa* (Who is there?), and they were expected to respond, *Fiiman* (free man). If they could not respond with the secret code, *Fiiman*, that meant they weren't really escapees, but instead, members of the Black Rangers, who were out to either discover where the Maroons lived to report back to the plantation owner, or they were there to recapture them and take them back to the plantation. As a result, leaders began to seek an alternative solution to disseminate the tumultuous environment. In Jamaica, settlers signed a peace treaty with Maroons in 1739,[57] and thus, the same would be sought in Suriname. The first treaty began with the Okanisi along the Maroni River in 1760, followed by the

---

[56] Van der Linden, Marcel. "The Okanisi: A Surinamese Maroon Community, C.1712–2010." *International Review of Social History* 60, no. 3 (2015): 463–90. doi:10.1017/S0020859015000383.

[57] Philip Wright, "War and Peace with the Maroons, 1730–1739," *Caribbean Quarterly* 16, no. 1 (1970): pp. 5-27, https://doi.org/10.1080/00086495.1970.11829035.

Saamaka along the Suriname River in 1762, and finally the Matawai along the Saramaka River in 1767.[58] These groups became known as the "pacified Bush Negroes," and Maroons not covered by the treaty were labeled as "non-pacified Bush Negroes." In Suriname, however, all the Maroon tribes did not agree to have a freedom treaty with the colonialists because they did not want to entertain the thought of forming alliances with them. According to legend, there have been some instances in which treaties were signed, and the colonialists would use power through trickery and bring the Maroons back into slavery or cause them to betray their own brothers that wanted to be free men in the beautiful country of Suriname.[59]

After the signed peace treaties, new runaways had to determine whether they would attempt to join the pacified Maroons, with the risk of being delivered back to their slave owners or form an alliance with the non-pacified Maroons. A third option was to retreat to a new location a further distance from the plantations. There were many factors in place, such as the difficulty in locating concealed Maroon grounds, risking the possibility of being killed by the non-pacified Maroons for fear of treachery, and others that made this decision-making crucial for survival.

Slavery, as we know in every country that had slavery, created a necessary secret internal language to communicate methods of survival and freedom that could not be interpreted or intercepted by slave masters and plantation dwellers. Communication would take place between the villages and alongside the rivers in various ways. In some villages, skillful drummers would transfer intricate messages through each beat in the wee hours of the night; other times, communication

---

[58] André R.M. Pakosie, "Maroon Leadership and the Surinamese State (1760–1990)," *The Journal of Legal Pluralism and Unofficial Law* 28, no. 37-38 (1996): pp. 263-277, https://doi.org/10.1080/07329113.1996.10756483.

[59] Eithne B. Carlin, *In and out of Suriname Language, Mobility and Identity* (Leiden, Netherlands: BRILL, 2015).

would be passed along through dugout canoes or oral dissemination.[60] Songs, however, were a primary code method that slaves would use to share their forbidden feelings and desires, longing for freedom, and plans of escape amidst fellow slaves. Even when slaves would leave the plantation, they would echo a song, with the colonialists utterly unaware of the power and strategy being communicated within its lyrics. The colonialists would think that the slaves were merely having fun as they would sing, "*Tamaa sonting miyaaw, Tamaa sonting malowe,*" which translated means, "Tomorrow we are leaving, tomorrow we will run away."[61]

As a toddler, I learned about this song created in slavery times between the 16th and 17th centuries. At a tender age, the song sounded both amusing and entertaining because it talked about going somewhere, but I had no clue of the hidden message in the song. The African slaves knew it was not just a song, but a hidden message they would share with their fellow African brethren. They knew they were about to embark on the journey of their lives, a journey between life and death. Can you imagine the power of this song in those days and all the emotions that went along with its melody? A slave's life hung at the crossroads, not knowing whether they would make it to their destination alive or if they would ever see their family and loved ones again.

Maroon Women

Because most Maroons were men, gender ratios remained distorted among the interior, giving a relative proportion of power to women and a steady rise to the matrilineal kinship structure. There are names of women chronicled throughout our history, as women were very influential during slavery time. The

---

[60] Olivia Maria Gomes da Cunha, Kenneth Bilby , and Rivke Jaffe, "'Real Bushinengué': Guianese Maroon Music in Transition," in *Maroon Cosmopolitics: Personhood, Creativity and Incorporation* (Leiden: Brill, 2019), pp. 330-349.

[61] Jacques Arends, *Language and Slavery: A Social and Linguistic History of the Suriname Creoles* (Philadelphia: John Benjamins Publishing, 2017).

matriline group became a strong organizational structure, sharing land rights, prayer stakes with ancestral sacrificial grounds, and other leadership tasks within the management of these rights. Women would also provide great counsel, namely the older, wise women of the tribe, instructing the villagers on where to go, what to do, and what not to do.[62]

The greatest power of Maroon women was that they were considered spiritual people. The Okanisi people lived a life saturated with the practice of religion. First, they had "the lower gods" that inhabited people for a specific mission. Then, the intermediate gods that were in control of day-to-day activity, were known as the Agedeonsu, Sweli Gadu, and Tati Ogii.[63] The Maroon women, emancipated and walking in freedom, exuded strength in the sense that they were spiritual, powerful, and confident in understanding the relationship between faith, protection, and healing. Maroon women made a covenant to cover and protect the people and upheld the covenant with strict standards. They were the ones to speak directly to the gods because they would not go into direct battle with the colonialists. They made a covenant god, giving them direct access to supernatural power.

A covenant in the Okanisi language and the Maroon language is called "Sweli."[64] You had the god of the Sweli, "the god of the covenant." The god of, when we say we will do this, we will do it. If you did not keep yourself to the ruling of that covenant, of that god, you would surely die. They would not tolerate anything less. As a person of faith, I know that any type of covenant made with

---

[62] Genia Julliette Lank Corinde, "Effective Collaboration between the Traditional Authority of the Maroon and the Central Government in Suriname: A Case Study at Resort Brownsweg" (University of Brasilia, 2017).

[63] Van der Linden, Marcel. "The Okanisi: A Surinamese Maroon Community, C.1712–2010." *International Review of Social History* 60, no. 3 (2015): 463–90. doi:10.1017/S0020859015000383.

[64] Kenneth Bilby, "Swearing by the Past, Swearing to the Future: Sacred Oaths, Alliances, and Treaties among the Guianese and Jamaican Maroons," *Ethnohistory* 44, no. 4 (1997): pp. 655-689, https://doi.org/10.2307/482884.

any god/s or spirits has repercussions if you break them. They say this is the god that brought them to freedom. When one would come into a covenant agreement with this god, there were certain protocols that you were required to uphold to the highest magnitude. If those protocols were abandoned, it was of dire consequence. Indeed, you would be killed, and thus, the covenant god was very effective and successful in practice.

In the stories of the Maroons and the Creoles passed down by ancestors, what I have been told is that the Creoles, the non-Maroon African descendants of Suriname, used to work together with the Maroons to help them flee from slavery. They were not enemies of each other, but more notably like comrades, working and co-existing together.[65] In the Maroon tribes, we have six tribes. First, the Saamaka, the Ndyuka or Okanisi, not Djuka, as many often inappropriately and disrespectfully mispronounce Ndyuka. The Pamaka is one of the smallest tribes. Aluku is a Maroon ethnic group living mainly on the riverbank in Maripasoula, located in southwest French Guiana. The group is sometimes called Boni, referring to the notorious leader, Bokilifu Boni. The Aluku was the new tribe Boni formed because he was not agreeing with the other fellow Okanisi people who signed the peace treaty, resulting in him fleeing with a group of freed Maroons.

The Aluku, or Boni, was known as being the volcanic nucleus of resistance. Within this book, I will refer to the name Boni as a person and Boni as a tribe of people. During the period of slavery and after the abolition of slavery, there were four people named Boni who were known as freedom fighters who strongly opposed the colonial regime. I will focus on the youngest one, Bokilifu Boni, who was killed by colonial soldiers. It is also important to note that none of these Bonis were enslaved, they all were born in freedom. These Maroons originated from Suriname; they are not from French Guiana.

---

[65] Bettina Migge, "Code-Switching and Social Identities in the Eastern Maroon Community of Suriname and French Guiana," *Journal of Sociolinguistics* 11, no. 1 (2007): pp. 53-73, https://doi.org/10.1111/j.1467-9841.2007.00310.x.

In the late 18th century, the Aluku occupied the region of Saint-Laurent-du-Maroni, Apatou, and Grand-Santi; the largest piece of the territory still occupied is called Fochi-ké (FirstCry), better known as Aluku, located in the region of Maripasoula. The Pamaka, Matawai, is another small group, not too small but smaller than the Okanisi and Saamaka. Finally, we have the smallest one among them, the Kwinti people. Each one of them has its own creole language. For example, the Okanesse speak Okanesse. The Saamaka speak Saamaka. The Matawai speak Matawai. The Kwinti speak Kwinti.[66] In my understanding, almost all of these tribes are related. The Saamaka and Okanisi are especially noted for their relational ties, as they all have the same name in the clan. Although there may be some slight differences, they all have clans divided into 12 units, which they call lo. The lo consists of several *bere* (pronounced as bee, as Maroons do not pronounce the "r"), which is the maternal house. Their way of heritage goes through the mother – they are of matrilineal lineage. The word *bere* means the womb or belly. The members within a *bere* are called the *mama osu pikin*. The mama *osu* includes the grandmother, daughters, granddaughters, and so forth, and the mama *bere* consists of the sisters and their children.[67]

Through the matrilineal structure, each position in the lo is determined. As such, they have chiefs and kings, and one can only become a king if their mother's sides have kings in it. Only one clan in the Okanisi tribe can become the Gaanman (king) of the Okanisi people, and it is called Otoo Clan – Otoo-Lo, as we call it.[68]

---

[66] Isabelle Léglise and Bettina Migge, "Language-Naming Practices, Ideologies, and Linguistic Practices: Toward a Comprehensive Description of Language Varieties," *Language in Society* 35, no. 03 (February 2006): pp. 313-339, https://doi.org/10.1017/s0047404506060155.

[67] Van der Linden, Marcel. "The Okanisi: A Surinamese Maroon Community, C.1712–2010." *International Review of Social History* 60, no. 3 (2015): 463–90. doi:10.1017/S0020859015000383.

[68] Kofi Yakpo and Robert Borges, "The Maroon Creoles of the Guianas: Expansion, Contact, and Hybridization," in *Boundaries and Bridges: Language Contact in Multilingual Ecologies* (Boston: Walter de Gruyter, 2017), pp. 87-128.

CHAPTER 5

FROM SLAVERY TO VICTORY:
THE NDYUKA PLIGHT TO FREEDOM

"Bigin fu lon na hesi waka"
(You have to walk before you run)

B etween 1794 and 1795, a group of African slaves revolted against Dutch authority and escaped from captivity, creating camps in the bush during that period.[69] The colonial regimes in the 1800s were still aware of the danger and threat posed by the revolution and the cruelty of the Dutch authorities that represented it.[70] The escaped slaves banded together, created armed camps, and commenced living independently. They were sometimes accepted as Bush Negroes. They encountered great odds to withstand harsh living conditions against the White attackers. They also went through difficult moments when it came to obtaining food. However, they kept increasing their population through reproduction.[71]

Enslaved individuals who managed to run away from their owners and vowed never to return to them found their permanent refuge from the devastating and dangerous life in swamps, plantations, forests, jungles, and mountains. In some instances, they attempted to live independently in either small groups or large communities if it guaranteed them freedom from the White interference.

---

[69] Howard, Rosalyn. "'Looking For Angola': An Archaeological and Ethnohistorical Search for a Nineteenth Century Florida Maroon Community and Its Caribbean Connections." *The Florida Historical Quarterly* 92, no. 1 (2013): pp. 32–68. http://www.jstor.org/stable/43487549.

[70] Gad J. Heuman, *Out of the House of Bondage: Runaways, Resistance and Marronage in Africa and the New World* (London: Routledge, 2016).

[71] Anne Rubenstein, Camilla Townsend, and Christopher Z. Hobson, "Revolted Negroes and the Devilish Principle: William Blake and Conflicting Visions of Boni's Wars in Surinam, 1772–1796," *Blake, Politics, and History*, 2015, pp. 273-298, https://doi.org/10.4324/9781315675176-16.

The Creation of the Bush Negroes and the Maroon Community

The Bush Negro community was born out of slavery. Enslaved individuals ran away from adverse living conditions, brutal punishment, and back-breaking heavy labor.[72] They existed in most parts of the Americas, and it is not a surprise that the two locations where they found their success, Suriname, and Jamaica, were known for their oppressive systems. Oppressive and heavy workloads could trigger a fight or a tug of war. Still, on most occasions, slaves preferred fleeing since they had already rebelled against their enslavement with violence and were aware of the possible consequences.[73]

It is crucial to differentiate between the Maroons and a vast number of slave runaways. Not all slaves that fled from bondage ended up becoming Bush Negroes. To be acknowledged as a Ndyuka, one had to go through several phases or stages.[74] Many runaway slaves could only manage to leave their plantations for a limited period and were either sought, captured, or willingly returned to their owners after a short period. In some instances, the owners put up advertisements indicating that they are willing to forgive their runaway slaves who returned willingly to their labor. The temporary absence that went on for an extended number of days was one way for laborers who were enslaved to express their discontent with their owners.

Moreover, few of the runaway slaves had the zeal and skills to fend for themselves in swamps or the woods, and once a slave thought of hunger, facing punishment when they returned to the plantation seemed better than starvation. However, Bush Negroes had no intention of going back to their employers or owners.[75] They established self-sufficient and independent communities that could not be governed by the systems created by Europeans in the Americas.

---

[72] Ibid.

[73] Heuman, *Out of the House of Bondage.*

[74] Rubenstein, Townsend, and Hobson, "Revolted Negroes and Devilish Principle."

[75] Heuman, *Out of the House of Bondage.*

There were also two forms of Bush Negroes which were acknowledged as Hinterland and Borderland Ndyukas. The Borderland formed their residence in swamps and forests between plantations. In other words, they found their home in liminal spaces that were owned by farmers legally, but which they never had time and resources to cultivate. The liminal spaces were close to the villages where slaves resided, and most of them knew they existed. On the other hand, Borderland Ndyukas had relatively easy access to material and basic needs from supplies emanating from the plantations, and they attempted to keep communication with friends and family.

However, the Borderland Ndyukas were vulnerable because of this support, making it easier for their owners to recapture them.[76] One reason why Hinterland Ndyukas made it harder for their owners to find them is because they went further away from their enslavement locations, deeper into the bush, woods, mountains, and swamps where they expected to start living their own life as a community. In simple terms, the difference between these two groups of Ndyukas is crucial since it assists in distinguishing between the individuals that sought to separate themselves from the world of enslavement and the ones that continued to interact with the day-to-day operations of slavery.[77]

Ethnic Roots of the Ndyuka

The ancestors of the Ndyuka were African slaves that managed to escape from coastal Suriname from the mid-17th to the late 18th centuries. After the culmination of nearly half a century of brutal punishment and guerrilla warfare against the European troops and colonial powers, the Maroons' independence was acknowledged by the signing of an agreement with the Dutch in the late 1760s.

---

[76] Ibid.

[77] Ibid.

The treaty permitted the Ndyuka to invade an extended part of the interior of Suriname that has been their homeland ever since.[78]

Ndyuka populations increased markedly around the 18th and 19th centuries. As a result, an increasing number of Ndyukas are now residing around the areas of Paramaribo, the capital city of Suriname.[79] Some of them were even trying to invade the eastern part of French Guiana, which is a practice that was born out of the survival tactics they achieved while living in swamps and deserted spaces between plantations. The Bush Negroes living in Suriname are known to be among the first former slaves to gain independence. Ultimately, they developed into the largest and most densely populated grouped slave descendants that ran away from captivity.[80] They enjoyed approximately a century of freedom before slavery was abolished in 1863. In the process, they established a culturally rich community life on their own in relative isolation, although they remained dependent on the coastal markets.[81]

Maroon communities are created in a quasi-military structure, which is a testament to their permanent readiness for military war. Their leaders were in most cases known by military titles, and the lieutenants were given roles to take responsibility for smaller bands capable of carrying out raids or marshal defenses in the community.[82] Moreover, the fortified town chosen by the Ndyuka individuals and the military tactics of the Maroons indicates that quite a number of them had military backgrounds in their native African countries.[83] It is acknowledged that no matter how many Bush Negroes or Ndyuka there were, they were not able to provide every basic need that the members of the community required. Metal

---

[78] Ibid.

[79] Ibid.

[80] Bruce Hoffman, "Exploring Biocultural Contexts: Comparative Woody Plant Knowledge of an Indigenous and Afro-American Maroon Community in Suriname, South America," *African Ethnobotany in the Americas*, 2012, pp. 335-393, https://doi.org/10.1007/978-1-4614-0836-9_13.

[81] Heuman, *Out of the House of Bondage.*

[82] Hoffman, "Exploring Biocultural Contexts," 340.

[83] Heuman, *Out of the House of Bondage.*

products, especially weapons, were in limited supply, as well as bullets for guns, gunpowder, finished garments, and clothing. As a result, to help acquire these products and services, some of the Ndyuka members were forced to raid plantations, where they managed to take domesticated animals in the process.[84] Another option that the Ndyuka employed was to trade either with enslaved individuals or the White people that were less privileged. Some Ndyuka groups interacted with the domestic community in such complex ways that some of the employers were willing to ignore their status. This strategy attracted less attention than those raiding plantations, and in the process, they also made their communities less vulnerable to attack.[85]

Ndyuka Community and the Enslaved

The Ndyukas emerged from the enslaved population, and some of them retained their family and other connections with the individuals who did not manage to escape. Because Ndyuka community members often hid around the plantations where their retained families were enslaved, the slave community played an instrumental role in supporting their basic needs.[86] They offered them clothing, food, and other necessities that could make their living conditions better, and in most instances, they ensured that the secreted runaway slaves knew of the plans of their masters. For this reason, there was either limited to no chance of Ndyuka settlements being attacked by surprise. In most cases, the invaders always found the Ndyuka settlements abandoned because they had received information about the attack beforehand. To the individuals that remained enslaved or failed to run away from their owners, the Ndyuka developed into mythic, heroic, and perhaps respectable figures among them. Furthermore, the retention and practice of African values and traditions, especially those associated with religion among the Ndyuka communities, ensured that they had a privileged position in slave

---

[84] Ibid.

[85] Ibid.

[86] Ibid.

societies with a large number of African slaves.[87] Most slaves believed that by fighting against the planter authority, the Ndyuka community was fulfilling the secret desires and wants of the less privileged members of their society.

The actions of the Ndyuka, along with other Maroons, put the enslaved in danger. They took what they required, although this could have affected the slaves adversely. Food and other necessities stolen from the plantations implied that the food available for those remaining was in limited supply or not enough. The kidnapping of Black or African women from the plantations was also challenging. They took women since they believed that they were crucial for increasing their population and the community's future, but taking them by force antagonized their families, friends, fathers, and husbands.[88] Irrespective of the way they conducted themselves, the Ndyuka individuals are remembered for being the first slaves to flee from captivity, which has raised their heroic status in the community.

The Relationship Between the Ndyuka and Amerindians

Bush Negroes either lived within or adjacent to the territories where Amerindians (indigenous people) were found. In some instances, the Whites managed to use Amerindians to forge an attack on the Ndyuka and return the slaves that wandered into their territory. However, their expectations were thwarted since most Amerindians would prefer to join forces with the Ndyuka. In most areas, including French Guiana, the Ndyuka community was biracial since they could infuse the African culture with the Amerindian culture.[89] Amerindians had to go through some rough spells and suffered a steep reduction in their population due to the introduction of European diseases. In the process, they found natural friends and allies in the runaway and self-emancipated Africans. One reason the Ndyuka Maroons were respected is that they lived in their village, paid

---

[87] Ibid.

[88] Ibid.

[89] Ibid.

tribute to Indian chiefs, and were governed by their administration for normal protection.[90] They also shared the same religious beliefs in Christianity and the power of their ancestors.

Figure 55 The Indigenous People are the First People of Suriname

For White masters, planters, governments, and militias, the Ndyuka community posed a particular challenge. Although the plantation owners were unwilling to lose the valuable property of the newly self-emancipated Africans, attempts to recapture them had to be evaluated against significant risks and efforts.[91] Ndyuka settlements were situated in remote and deliberately inaccessible areas. The days that the White mercenaries hunted the Ndyuka and

---

[90] Ibid.

[91] Ibid.

other Maroons were considered days lost from taking care of the plantation, and the remaining slaves could damage crops and their positive net revenues either through willful or accidental vandalism. Some of them even took advantage of the disappearance of the masters to flee away from the plantations.[92] The woods, swamps, and mountains were instrumental in forming formidable environments full of adverse fauna that preyed on unwary individuals. There was no chance that many Whites ventured anywhere around those locales, except in situations when they were required to, so that those areas, in effect, developed into spaces that were occupied and traversed only by Africans. Some masters tried to ignore the activities of the Ndyuka, especially if their plantation raids did not cause too much trouble. However, when the runaway and self-emancipated Africans' activities became audacious, and the losses incurred regarding food, livestock, and additional escapees became too severe to ignore, the White masters were forced to act.[93] The Ndyuka individuals attacked by the White mercenaries had only two choices, either to fight or run away. Flight was the most common choice if they were outgunned or outnumbered. Since they knew their settlements better than the Whites, they preferred running away and toward these areas. To counter the benefits of local knowledge of the terrain and land held by the runaway and self-emancipated Africans, some White authorities looked to the Amerindians for help.[94]

How the Runaway Captives Were Recognized

Given the challenges of permanently eradicating the Ndyuka and other Maroon communities as soon as they settled in French Guiana and other locations, some colonial authorities attempted a different approach. For instance, having tried and failed to deal with the extensive Maroon band that resided near Vera Cruz, the Mexican authorities decided to enter a treaty with one of the Maroon

---

[92] Ibid.

[93] Ibid.

[94] Ibid.

leaders known as the Yanga. In doing so, they accepted the free status associated with the Maroons that were governed by his power and allowed them to live freely in their town.[95] Based on this treaty, the runaway slaves from captivity revolutionized the face of African American communities living in the United States.[96] In situations where both parties respected the agreement, there was a great chance that both the Ndyuka and the other runaway slaves could command some level of respect and gradually assimilate into the extensive population through other social interactions and trade. Through such treaties, it was also possible for the Ndyuka people to maintain their distance and isolation and, in the process, minimize any implications of what its existence might cause to the White society.[97]

On the other hand, treaties could be broken, which could result in renewed hostilities. Some Ndyuka individuals were lax in the pursuit of runaways, proven by the fact that they accepted fugitives into their society to help increase their population or boost their numbers. In contrast, others continued raiding plantations and stealing items and supplies. As the population increased, the Ndyuka community realized that their isolation from the other communities and the disappearance of slaves was due to the expanding colonial settlements.[98]

The policy of the Dutch administration revolved around assimilation. In other words, the traditional customs, languages, values, and traditions had to give over to the Dutch language, law, and way of thinking. The introduction of compulsory education in 1876 was one of the most instrumental elements at the core of this policy.[99] The collaboration of the Ndyuka community and the Dutch administration implied that assimilation had to pave a way for overt ethnic

---

[95] Raymond T. Smith, *The Negro Family in British Guiana: Family Structure and Social Status in the Villages* (New York, NY: Routledge, 2013).

[96] Heuman, *Out of the House of Bondage.*

[97] Smith, *The Negro Family in British Guiana.*

[98] Heuman, *Out of the House of Bondage.*

[99] Ibid.

diversity. In contrast to the traditional beliefs of the light-skinned population, the Surinamese government acknowledges the Asian cultural marriages and traditions. As a result, the Second World War caused serious implications to the social-economic structure.

The presence of the United States troops to help offer protection to transport routes and bauxite mines resulted in an improvement in the population in urban and rural districts of Paramaribo and other mining centers.[100] As a result, the collaboration of the Maroons made Paramaribo a multiethnic city, and it also reduced the population of light-skinned Creoles. Suriname also developed into an autonomous section of the Netherlands Kingdom.[101] Maroons of French Guiana and Suriname, which descend from the Bush Negroes, are the two hemispheres of the extensive Maroon population. Since the 1970s and 1980s, they are also the most politically, economically, and culturally independent of all the runaway Africans in the Americas. They are also among the most heavily assaulted.[102]

---

[100] Ibid.

[101] Smith, *The Negro Family in British Guiana.*

[102] Heuman, "Out of the House of Bondage."

CHAPTER 6

APPRENTICESHIP SYSTEM

"Mi na wan uman anga wan sisa no?"

(Am I not a woman and sister?)

M illions of slaves were traded across the Atlantic Ocean into the Caribbean region in earlier centuries. This trade was called the Transatlantic Slave Trade. These people who were enslaved rebelled against slavery right up until emancipation in 1834.

Figure 56 Map of The Caribbean

Numerous slave revolts occurred in the 18th and 19th centuries. Some notable ones recorded in history were Tacky's rebellion in Jamaica during the 1760s; the Haitian Revolution in 1791; Fedon's revolution in Grenada in 1795; the 1816 Barbados slave revolt that was spearheaded by Bussa; and the 1831 slave revolt in Jamaica led by Sam Sharpe. The British slave trade officially ended in 1807, and the buying and selling of slaves became an illegal activity. Although this was the case, activities that occurred after the abolition of slavery suggested that slavery had not ended. Slavery in British Caribbean islands did not end until August 1, 1834, after legislation was passed in 1833. When slavery was abolished, a period of apprenticeship started.

Apprenticeship System

The apprenticeship system aimed to facilitate a smooth and easy transition from slavery to freedom. It was also used to ensure sugar production by guaranteeing that the planters had a labor force for up to six years following the abolition of slavery. The program aimed at allowing both the planters and the freedmen to adjust to the concept of freedom and its demands. The apprenticeship system was based on the concept that slaves were not ready for freedom because of numerous reasons. These reasons included that Blacks did not have enough money to provide for their basic needs. They also said that this system was necessary because the Blacks did not have the skills needed to survive or find work. During the apprenticeship systems, the plantation owners offered Blacks jobs on the plantations, housing, and a wage they claimed was reasonable.[103]

Since most of the work available was on the same plantations where formerly enslaved people worked, they were still not treated fairly. Some described the apprenticeship program as a new form of slavery in the Caribbean. Wages were low, and people did not have enough legal rights to land. In most cases, freedmen had to rent houses to live in, and the rent and taxes were high. Unemployment levels were also very high during this time. An example that highlights the desperate situations of these slaves was the rebellion that occurred in Jamaica, where the working classes protested about such deplorable conditions. The events that unfolded across the Caribbean started to prove that an anti-slavery movement had not succeeded in ending the war against slavery because these so-called freedmen were not much better off under the new apprenticeship system.[104]

---

[103] Pieter Emmer, "Between Slavery and Freedom: The Period of Apprenticeship in Suriname (Dutch Guiana), 1863–1873," *Slavery & Abolition* 14, no. 1 (1993): pp. 87-113, https://doi.org/10.1080/01440399308575085.

[104] Gad Heuman, "Riots and Resistance in the Caribbean at the Moment of Freedom," *Slavery & Abolition* 21, no. 2 (2000): pp. 135-149, https://doi.org/10.1080/01440390008575309.

Other conditions that betrayed the concept of the apprenticeship system gave rise to much concern. Across the Caribbean, mental health institutions often suffered from poor standards of care, overcrowding, and patient neglect. There was an abuse of the system because forced labor persisted, and persons imprisoned for various reasons were subject to floggings. Formerly enslaved people received no compensation and had limited representation in the laws.[105] Ex-slaves began protesting the apprenticeship system and demanded immediate, unconditional freedom. They refused to accept the need for any form of transition from slavery and supervised working conditions because they had gained needed experience during slavery and the years they spent as apprentices.[106] A new era was now dawning because these freed slaves now wanted to focus on their own family life and choose their own work hours, employers, and the type of work they performed. A small number of apprentices tried to buy their freedom, but very few were successful in doing so. The price for freedom was extremely high, so they remained in their deplorable working conditions. Across the West Indies, many of those who were called apprentices refused to continue working and went on strikes. This protest did create change in some cases because in Trinidad, for example, apprentices were afforded a five-day workweek, and workers were paid for any work they did on a Saturday.[107]

The ex-slaves started a campaign against the apprenticeship system. There were petitions to abolish this practice, and they eventually won the battle to end

[105] The National Archives, "Caribbean Histories Revealed," The National Archives (The National Archives, Kew, Surrey TW9 4DU, November 10, 2006), https://www.nationalarchives.gov.uk/caribbeanhistory/slavery-negotiating-freedom.htm.

[106] Spence, Caroline Quarrier. 2014. Ameliorating Empire: Slavery and Protection in the British Colonies, 1783-1865. Doctoral dissertation, Harvard University.

[107] David B. Ryden, "Revolutionary Emancipation: Slavery and Abolitionism in the British West Indies, Written by Claudius K. Fergus," *New West Indian Guide* 90, no. 1-2 (2016): pp. 86-88, https://doi.org/10.1163/22134360-09001004.

the apprenticeship program.[108] Slaves had a choice whether to work on these plantations or not, but some had other dreams of owning their own land and working for themselves, which they did. This was the case in Jamaica in particular, but on other Caribbean islands, where there was no vacant land to farm, many had no other choice than to continue working on plantations for their former owner for low wages.

Figure 57 The Famous Banner for the Campaign Against Apprenticeship, Anti-Slavery International

The Indentured Workers

In many Caribbean islands, apprenticeship did not prove to be an incentive for enough ex-slaves to continue working on the plantations. Higher wages instead helped the ex-slaves to move away from the plantations because they could now afford to do so financially. At a point, the cost of labor on plantations across the Caribbean made it easier to just hire workers from places in Europe and

---

[108] Richard Huzzey, *Freedom Burning: Anti-Slavery and Empire in Victorian Britain* (Ithaca: Cornell University Press, 2012).

Asia. They had first turned to Africa for hired workers, but this was futile because of their reputation for enslaving the Africans. So planters started recruiting workers from Europe, mainly in Spain and Portugal, in addition to some Germans.[109] Other migrant laborers in the Caribbean came from British India and Spain. These laborers were bonded to work for a certain period for wages that were negotiated on the plantations. Because the ex-slaves increasingly refused to sign labor contracts and withdrew from permanent positions as resident field laborers, this move to import new laborers was necessary if their plantations were to be kept alive. For those freedmen who opted to work on these plantations, they were required to provide a full week's labor because the planters only wanted those kinds of freedmen to live on their estates. Others were required to either leave or pay rent or were evicted.

The replacement of slaves and freedmen by indentured immigrants occurred over time. For example, in the British Caribbean, the first set of indentured laborers arrived after the end of the apprenticeship, while others arrived in the Caribbean during later periods. The system of indentured workers resulted in a lot of abuse and was abolished in the early part of the 20th century. In fact, it was reported that the "indentured laborers from Asia were so badly treated they could not possibly succeed in building a new and successful existence in the Caribbean."[110] After indenture, Indians and Africans struggled to own land and create their own communities.

After indentured labor was abolished, the political and citizenship status of newly freed slaves was discussed among colonial authorities and members of Parliament. Other reforms started to be made where missionaries, clergymen, and

---

[109] Michael Adas, "A New System of Slavery: The Export of Indian Labour Overseas, 1830–1920. By Hugh Tinker. London: Oxford University Press, 1974. Pp. XVI, 432 + 18 Plates. £5.75.," *The Journal of Economic History* 34, no. 4 (1974): pp. 1062-1063, https://doi.org/10.1017/s0022050700089695.

[110] Howard Temperley, ed., *After Slavery: Emancipation and Its Discontents* (Portland, OR: Frank Cass, 2000).

magistrates tried to change these free slaves morally, culturally, and spiritually from their cultural habits. For example, they would encourage ex-slaves to form legal marriage unions and adapt to the nuclear family standard. These missionaries also established schools and persuaded the freed people to adopt Christianity.

After the end of the indenture era, during the mid-19th century, the Caribbean's economy began to fail. This was because the price of sugar began to fall.

Figure 58 Example of Indentured Workers/Laborers Arriving in Suriname

Formation of CARICOM

The Caribbean Community (CARICOM) is an organization of 15 Caribbean nations and dependencies. It was established on August 1, 1973, to replace the Caribbean Free Trade Association, which ceased to exist on May 1, 1974.[111] The main goal of CARICOM is to promote economic integration and cooperation

---

[111] "History of the Caribbean Community," CARICOM, July 23, 2020, https://caricom.org/history-of-the-caribbean-community/.

among its member states. This ensures equity among them and coordination of foreign policy, major economic policies, and development planning.

CARICOM operates as a regional single market for many of its members (CARICOM Single Market (CSME)). CARICOM was established by the signing of the Treaty of Chaguaramas that took place in Trinidad. This cooperation among these groups of islands in the Caribbean that were once colonized facilitates free trade among them as well as other types of partnership.[112]

Figure 59 Signing of the Treaty of Chaguaramas in Trinidad to Establish CARICOM

Goals of the CSME

The CSME seeks to promote opportunities for growth and development of member Caribbean states by creating a single economic space where competitive goods and services are produced. It is at the heart of CARICOM's economic integration. Some of the major outcomes of the CSME since its formation include the removal of the work-permit system. Citizens of CARICOM member states can seek employment in any of the countries that are signatories to the treaty and accept these job offers without a work permit. There is a Certificate of CARICOM Skills Qualification that is accepted right across all the CARICOM member states. Creating the Caribbean Court of Justice was aimed at interpreting and applying the Treaty that established CARICOM and settled disputes.[113]

---

[112] Ibid.

[113] Ibid.

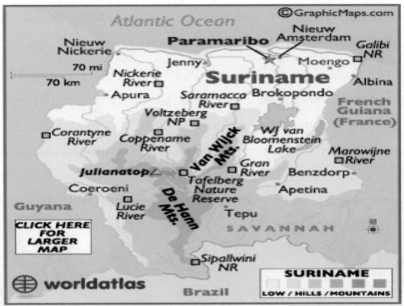
Figure 60 Map of Suriname

Different Era That Blacks Experienced After the Abolition of Slavery In Suriname

Suriname falls under Dutch colonial rule. Governors Mauritius and Crommeling successfully made peace treaties with some Maroon tribes, but some tribes attacked the European settlements. One of the best-known Maroon tribe leaders of the second half of the 18th century was Boni, who led revolutions against slavery. The French Revolution of 1789 led to the abolition of slavery in Suriname's eastern neighbor, French Guiana, which affected the Surinamese plantation owners.[114]

Ten-Year Mandatory Probation Program

There was a period of turmoil between the end of the 17th and the beginning of the 18th century in Suriname. After this period, there was a flourishing

---

[114] Natasha Alexander, *Suriname Country Study Guide* (Washington, DC: International Business Publications, USA, 2005).

agricultural sector in Suriname. There was a great demand for laborers, and most of the work on the plantations was done by African slaves. The slaves were not treated kindly. Suriname, in particular, had a bad reputation in the Caribbean region concerning slave treatment. As a result, many slaves ran away from the plantations into the jungle. Of note is the fact that the runaway slaves created a new and unique culture that was self-reliant and successful. They established several independent tribes that lived in different areas of the rainforest. These runaway slaves often returned to attack the plantations, which made the lives of the plantation owners miserable. These attacks were often deadly for the plantation owners and their families. The Maroons would frequently raid the plantations to recruit new members and get women, weapons, food, and other supplies. To ease the problem, Governors Mauritius and Crommeling managed to make peace treaties with some Maroon tribes while other tribes attacked the plantations. The slave trade was abolished by the English in 1808 and improved the position of the Surinamese slaves. Ten years before the abolition of slavery, the plantation owners started importing migrant laborers to fill the gap that the fleeing of the Maroons left to be plugged. The first laborers were Chinese. The Chinese, however, immediately left the plantations after their five-year obligatory contract working period ended. They were unable to bear the cruelties of the plantation owners. These deadly attacks on the planters and their families continued, and after several unsuccessful campaigns against the Maroons, the European authorities decided to cease the practice.[115]

Slavery in Suriname was abolished in 1863; however, the slaves were not completely removed from the plantations until 1873, which amounted to ten years

---

[115] New World Encyclopedia contributors, "Suriname," *New World Encyclopedia,* https://www.newworldencyclopedia.org/p/index.php?title=Suriname&oldid=1030565 (accessed March 25, 2022).

after.[116] This period is not called the apprenticeship system, unlike other Caribbean neighbors who experienced an era called the apprenticeship system. They were required to work on the plantations for minimal pay and without state-sanctioned torture.

How the Mandatory Ten Years Worked

The ten-year mandatory work period mirrored the apprenticeship system, which was designed to facilitate a smooth and easy transition from slavery to freedom...at least that is what the plantation owners said. Like the apprenticeship system, another objective of this system was to ensure that the continued production of sugar on the sugar plantations was guaranteed. Traditionally, in other Caribbean countries, the apprenticeship program lasted for eight years, but the mandatory transition system lasted for ten years in Suriname. The other difference with Suriname's ten-year mandatory probation program is that while it was optional for slaves in other Caribbean countries to choose whether or not they wanted to take up paid labor on these plantations, in Suriname, it was mandatory. Another reason they went through this period in Suriname, like other Caribbean countries, is that the planters wanted to ensure they had a labor force for up to six years following the abolition of slavery. Without a labor force, their businesses would perish, and so they mandated that the slaves stay on for this so-called transition period.[117]

The mandatory ten-year period also had other objectives. The slave masters claimed that the program would allow both themselves and the freed slaves to adjust to the concept of freedom and its demands. The ten-year mandatory probation period that mirrored the apprenticeship system was based on the

---

[116] Rosemarijn Hoefte, "A Passage to Suriname? The Migration of Modes of Resistance by Asian Contract Laborers," *International Labor and Working-Class History* 54 (1998): pp. 19-39, https://doi.org/10.1017/s0147547900006190.

[117] Ibid.

concept that slaves were not ready for freedom for numerous reasons, which included the concern that the Blacks did not have enough money to provide for their basic needs. The planters felt that the freed slaves would still be dependent on them for sustenance. Another reason they claimed that this period was necessary, was because the plantation owners believed the slaves did not have the needed skills to survive or find work. This, despite working on the plantations doing the same work for many years before this era.

Like other Caribbean countries, the plantation owners made the slaves work on the plantations for ten years, only this time they were paid wages. The wages were extremely low during this period, but the slaves were not free to do otherwise. They were still abused by the slave masters and the system of slavery.

Of note is that during this period of mandatory state supervision, the slaves could legally obtain weekly portions of food as well as clothes that should have lasted them up to a year, or a minimum of half of a year. The slaves under the law were entitled to a certain standard of housing and medical care under this system, and they could complain about any breach of these laws. Slaves under the mandatory state supervision period were free to move to different plantations to work after their contracts ended, and they had the option to sign work contracts that spanned from three months to one year.

As soon as they became truly free, the slaves largely abandoned the plantations where they had suffered for several generations and moved to cities like Paramaribo.[118] Another contrast with Suriname and the rest of the Caribbean was that across the West Indies, in most cases, many of those who were called apprentices refused to continue working and went on strikes. In Suriname, the slaves were not engaged in planned protests.

During the ten-year mandatory state supervision period in Suriname, the plantation owners began to become involved in the importation of indentured

---

[118] Ibid.

workers. An indentured worker in Suriname, as in other places in the Caribbean that imported them, was an employee who was bound by a signed contract to work for a particular employer for a fixed time. This period in Suriname was for at least 5 years.[119] The planters in Suriname started taking indentured workers from the Dutch East Indies. These were mostly Chinese, hence the creation of the Chinese Surinamese population in Suriname. After emancipation in Suriname on July 1, 1863, the planters started importing workers from India and other places.[120]

While there was some importation of indentured laborers, work on the plantations remained uncertain until the very end of the period of state supervision. Originally, the emancipation law had contained a clause stipulating that the colonial government would be involved in the organization of large-scale immigration of free laborers into Suriname. Parliament, however, decided against any official participation in such an immigration scheme. After much discussion, it was decided that the colonial authorities were allowed to draw on an 'Immigration Fund' enabling them to subsidize the cost of transportation of privately imported indentured laborers. In 1870, the Dutch government started allowing more immigration of indentured laborers from India every year.

---

[119] Rosemarijn Hoefte, "Control and Resistance: Indentured Labor in Suriname," *New West Indian Guide/Nieuwe West-Indische Gids* 61, no. 1-2 (January 1987): pp. 1-22, https://doi.org/10.1163/13822373-90002053.

[120] "History of Suriname," Encyclopædia Britannica (Encyclopædia Britannica, inc.), accessed March 25, 2022, https://www.britannica.com/place/Suriname/History.

Figure 61 Monument of "Baba and Mai" that Commemorates the Arrival of the First British Indian Immigrants in Suriname

Although there were many negatives associated with not being completely free, some positives came out of the ten years of compulsory labor and supervision by the state. The slaves were able to save some money from what they had earned over the ten years of state supervision. They were able to physically prepare for Emancipation Day. They used some of the money they had saved to buy new clothes and shoes. They started their journey towards financial independence during the probation period. The probation period also paved the way for Suriname's independence. Not all ex-slaves were willing to continue to work after emancipation. Some refused to go back to work. Only the personal intervention of the colonial governor himself made them change their minds. The work schedule of the slavery period had been changed by the law concerning emancipation. The law stipulated that the ex-slaves working as field hands on the plantations were obliged to enter into contracts with the employer of their choice for at least one year as of October 1863. The same law stipulated that during the period between July 1st and October 1st, 1863, the ex-slaves should work four days per week at two-thirds of the wages according to the rate of wage payments for free laborers as set by the colonial government in 1861.[121] That meant that the ex-slaves moved from a six-day workweek to a four-day workweek and that they were facing a six-day workweek again in the immediate future. Because of this, many slaves must have considered the period of compulsory labor contracts after October 1, 1863, as a return to the days of slavery. It certainly induced the ex-slaves to postpone the signing of contracts to the last possible moment.

Many slaves used the gap between July and October 1863 to search for employment outside their own plantations. The planters, the missionaries, and the colonial authorities all complained about this very disturbing trend. This was, however, stimulated by some of the planters because some of them had openly said that they could not afford to pay the set wages. The governor of Suriname estimated that around 10,000 freedmen were in danger of being unemployed after emancipation. To offer temporary employment, the colonial government took over two sugar plantations during the period between July 1st and October 1st, 1863."[122] Many ex-slaves felt that the only way they could use their freedom was by moving to another plantation since they were obliged to remain in plantation agriculture.

There was a tendency among the freed slaves to change employers frequently, immediately after the ten-year probation period ended, which caused the planters to complain bitterly. Many lived in constant fear that all or almost all of their laborers might move away when their labor contracts expired right before the sugar crop was due to be harvested." The ex-slaves, however, were said to move away from the plantations on which they used to live "because they disliked the management."[123]

---

[121] Michael Twaddle, ed., *The Wages of Slavery: From Chattel Slavery to Wage Labour in Africa, the Caribbean, and England* (London: Routledge, 2015).

[122] Ibid.

[123] Ibid.

The Dutch abolished slavery in 1863, long after the British abolished it. Although the slaves were freed, they had to continue working on their plantations on a contract basis and were not released until 1873, ten years later. The only difference was that they were paid a wage during that period. When slavery was abolished in Suriname, workers began to be imported from other places to fill the need for laborers on the plantations. The owners of the plantations started by importing laborers from other continents. The first people who arrived to work on the plantations in Suriname after the abolition of slavery were Chinese. Before their arrival, however, some Dutch farmers were taken to Suriname to start small farms, but this attempt did not save the agricultural importance of Suriname. In fact, half of the Dutch farmers died within a year, and the Chinese immediately left the plantations after their five-year obligatory working period ended.

From 1873 to 1916, many other laborers were taken to Suriname to work on the plantations. Jews, Portuguese, Spaniards, and Italians were among the people who came to work on sugar plantations in Suriname after the abolition of slavery. These workers included Indians who were also required to work on the plantations for some years; then, they were able to return to India or prolong their contract when it expired. It is said that about 37,000 Indians were imported to Suriname "before a movement in India led by Mahatma Gandhi stopped this immigration in 1916."[124] Workers were also imported from Indonesia. Most of them left the plantations after their contract ended and started small farms in Suriname. This movement caused the plantations to lose their importance to the economy of the country, and a drastic decline of the number of sugar plantations declined from 80 in 1863 to 4 in 1940.

---

[124] Das Tania Gupta and Verene Shepherd, "Prelude to Settlement: Indians as Indentured Labourers," in *Race and Racialization: Essential Readings* (Toronto: Canadian Scholars, 2018), pp. 155-156.

CHAPTER 7

RISING FROM THE ASHES

MALOGASSI

"Opo taampu da yu kaka futu"

(Rise up and stand your ground)

ormerly known as Dutch Guiana, Suriname became independent on November 25, 1975. A Creole sergeant named Desi Bouterse, who was also a physical education instructor in the Dutch-Surinamese army, joined a newly formed Surinamese national army. Five years after independence, he led a military coup against the civilian government of Prime Minister Henck Arron in February 1980 that turned Suriname into a socialist state. From 1980 to 1987, the military continued to control the state with a succession of nominally civilian administrations that held on to power until 1987, when they yielded to mounting international pressure and held a democratic election.[125]

The year 1980 was an unforgettable year for me. It was a Monday morning, on February 25, 1980, and my two brothers and I were getting ready for school. We had just put on our school uniforms and were preparing for our 30-minute walk to school when right before 7:00 am, we heard loud sounds. These sounds were coming from the downtown Paramaribo area. These sounds were not familiar to us. They were loud and had a peculiar sound, like some type of large fireworks...that was all we could compare it with. These loud sounds were frightening and non-stop. We did not have a television, so we could not know what was going on outside. Then there was a loud knock on our back door. It was my brother-in-law, Lloyd, he was in the army. He came through the door very quickly, dressed fully in his uniform, and urged us not to leave the house. "Listen to me!" he said, "Nobody leaves this house! Mom, you cannot leave the house

---

[125] Scott B. MacDonald, "Insurrection and Redemocratization in Suriname? The Ascendancy of the 'Third Path,'" *Journal of Interamerican Studies and World Affairs* 30, no. 1 (1988): pp. 105-132, https://doi.org/10.2307/165791.

right now, and guys, you cannot leave the house to go to school because there is a war downtown, and we do not know what will happen here."

Not knowing the magnitude of the destruction taking place downtown to our historic buildings, my brothers and I were excited. We did not have to go to school; that was always cause for celebration. Later, my household learned that innocent people had been killed and historic buildings destroyed.

The following year, due to the tumultuous unrest still brimming in Paramaribo, my mother shipped me and my young brothers off to La Providencia Boarding School in Abadoe Kondre in hopes of better security and opportunity. The village of Abadoe Kondre is located 5 kilometers (approximately 3 miles) west of the bauxite town of Moengo, inside the district of Mowijne. This is where we would spend the next five years, only to come home and visit family one weekend a month, and on holidays. The boarding school became our second home and our new norm.

Bouterse started to rule the country as the new autocrat and head of the military council. He then promoted himself to the highest rank in the Surinamese National Army as Lieutenant Colonel. Bouterse proceeded to dismantle parliament, suspend the constitution, and declare a state of emergency in the country to impose his self-appointed regime. He then created a special tribunal to prevent the previous government from reclaiming power.[126]

In 1986, my brothers and I were home for the holidays and were getting ready to go back to boarding school when we got word that the boarding school had closed, and we would not be able to go back. We would soon find out that this was because the place we considered our second home had now become a war zone. We would also learn that some of our fellow students had been killed during this war. These were kids we were so close to we considered ourselves brothers.

---

[126] Ivelaw L. Griffith, *The Re-Emergence of Suriname's Désiré (DESI) Bouterse: Political Acumen and Geopolitical Anxiety* (Miami, FL: Applied Research Center, Florida International University, 2011).

This brought a complete transition in our lives because we were not sure if we would ever see our friends from the boarding school again.

In June 1986, Bouterse unleashed his full artillery, complete with tanks, on the defenseless village of Mungo-tapu, the village of my grandfather.[127] In the weeks and months that followed, similar violent actions were taken against other Ndyuka villages, including Mola-kondre, the village of my grandmother, and Moiwana. All these villages were near our boarding school, which made the whole area surrounding our school a war zone. As a matter of fact, the entire district of Marowijne became a war zone. Violence against the Maroons continued to soar, and Moiwana became one of the villages that were hit the hardest.

Figure 62 Moiwana Monument to the Victims of the Moiwana Massacre of 1986 in the District of Marowijne, Suriname

On November 29, 1986, the army of Suriname attacked Moiwana. Moiwana was the hometown of Ronnie Brunswijk, who was a member of the Surinamese Army and former personal bodyguard for Desi Bouterse in the 1980s. Thirty-nine

---

[127] Franszoon Adiante, "The Suriname Maroon Crisis," Cultural Survival Quarterly Magazine (Cultural Survival, December 1, 1988), https://www.culturalsurvival.org/publications/cultural-survival-quarterly/suriname-maroon-crisis.

people from the village were brutally murdered, mostly women and children. Houses were burned down, including the house of Ronnie Brunswijk, and the village was destroyed. Over a hundred people fled across the border to take refuge in French Guiana. For years to come during the war, French Guiana became the destination for other refugees, including some of my family members. The International Court of Human Rights ordered the government to pay millions of U.S. dollars in compensation to the over 130 survivors of the Moiwana village attacks. This civil war had dire effects on the Blacks in Suriname. The civil war was based on contempt. Many urban Surinamese viewed Maroons with contempt. Bloodshed against the Maroons ensued, and men, women, and children were killed brutally through bombing attacks. Many Maroons were left homeless and lost their loved ones.[128] At the same time, many of the Maroons who opposed the war on their villages acted, and the prominent leader was Ronnie Brunswijk. Brunswijk left Bouterse and the army and formed the Surinamese Liberation Army, which he described as the "Jungle Commando." Together, with his Commandos, they persisted against the national military under Bouterse. His mission was to gain recognition and rights for the Maroon minorities of the interior and free the Surinamese people from the military dictatorship of Bouterse. That is why he called this civil war the "Surinamese Interior War," which endured from 1986 until 1990. In 1987, a new civilian constitution was approved. The blacks became refugees and lived in an atmosphere where soldiers came and rounded up women and children and took them to other parts of the jungle to be shot.[129] During this period, there were over 10,000 refugees who fled to French Guiana to seek refuge. Even though many lives were shed due to Brunswijk's perseverance, they reached a peace agreement in 1991 between the National Army and Jungle Commando to cease the war.

---

[128] Ibid.

[129] Ibid.

This did not last. That same year, the military again overthrew the civilian leadership of Suriname, and a coalition of four major parties formed a democratically elected government. Up to 2005, the coalition government had expanded to include eight parties in power. This coalition stayed in power until 2010, when the Suriname voters reverted to military leadership, bringing back Desi Bouterse, which was vehemently opposed to the forming of coalitions to grip leadership and stay in power.

In 1999, Bouterse was sentenced by a Dutch court to eleven years in prison for smuggling up to 400kg of cocaine into the country. However, in 2012, the Surinamese parliament challenged this court ruling by passing a controversial law that granted Bouterse immunity for the criminal activities that he was alleged to have committed during military rule, and he did not face trial or any prison sentence.[130] In 2015, President Bouterse was re-elected to power unopposed. It is also important to note that most Surinamese political parties are formed along ethnic lines.[131]

Figure 63 Desi D. Bouterse, Former President of Suriname

---

[130] "Desi Bouterse: Suriname President Gets 20 Years in Jail for Murder," BBC News (BBC, November 30, 2019), https://www.bbc.com/news/world-latin-america-50611555.

[131] "The World Factbook."

Despite having an election in 1987, most Black people in Suriname were left out of the process. To be more precise, one report stated, "As for what has happened with the Maroons and in the countryside, we couldn't care less." This resulted in the Maroons having no representation in the new government. The goal was to eradicate the Blacks from Suriname. It is said that Bouterse stated that he "would not rest until he eliminated all the Maroons from Suriname."[132] Despite the threat of Bouterse to the Maroon people, the future existence of the Maroon people remains very bright. Today, Maroons contribute largely to the development of Suriname's interior part and the entire economy of Suriname.

While Bouterse was in power in 2019, he was found guilty of planning and ordering the extrajudicial execution of fifteen political opponents in 1982.[133] A panel of three female judges consequently sentenced Bouterse in a military court to twenty years in prison. The president previously denied all the allegations claiming that the victims were trying to escape Fort Zeelandia, the colonial area fortress in Paramaribo. Among these victims were scholars, lawyers, union leaders, and journalists, some of Suriname's brightest minds. Bouterse learned about the sentence while he was on an official state visit to China. It was unclear what would happen upon his arrival back to Suriname. The judges did not issue an arrest order to avoid potential civil unrest in the country that could ultimately lead to civil war. His lawyer, Irvin Kanhai, did not waste time appealing the decision of the judges, stating that it was a political verdict. Right now, in Suriname, it is unclear what the future of Bouterse looks like.

Current Situation

The current situation in Suriname promises to go in the right direction with the current administration. In the May 2020 election, the people selected a new

---

[132] Richard Price, "Executing Ethnicity: The Killings in Suriname," *Cultural Anthropology* 10, no. 4 (1995): pp. 437-471, https://doi.org/10.1525/can.1995.10.4.02a00010.

[133] BBC, "Suriname President in Jail for Murder."

government under the leadership of President Chandrikapersad "Chan" Santokhi and Vice President Ronnie Brunswijk. This new administration has promised to prosper the economy and to bring restoration after the grim situation that plagued the country.

Figure 64 Ronnie Brunswijk, Vice President of Suriname

The question is, "Is there hope for Suriname's economy to flourish as it is promised by the new administration?" Based on Suriname's history, there is a long-standing history of patriotism among the Surinamese people, both within the country and abroad. With that drive and love for the country, I believe prosperity is within reach. To achieve this goal, there must be ongoing cooperation between the private sector and the government.

Even though the new administration has vowed to establish prosperity for the nation and country, the majority of Surinamese people are very skeptical because of their experiences with governments that did not keep their promises. Given the fact that Suriname is such a small country with a small population consisting of approximately 500,000 people, the infrastructure is in constant transition. As a result of such inconsistency, there is a continuous challenge to create stability in the country. There is hope, however, and stability is possible for the country and its economy. With transparent leadership, all the natural resources, investors, and support from other countries, Suriname can rise above its challenges and indeed be the gem of the Caribbean and South America.

A Comparison of Events or Experiences of The Eras Following the Abolition of Slavery Among the United States of America, The Caribbean, And Suriname

Who knew, unless they read the history of these three places, that The United States of America, the Caribbean, and Suriname had one thing in common? Yes, the slave trade affected all three territories. There was slavery in the United States of America as much as there was in the Caribbean and Suriname. Based on the information presented earlier, we see noticeable comparisons of the post-slavery eras in these three places. A close examination of the events that occurred in these regions after slavery confirms that the effect of the slave trade impacted individuals' long-term and even generations that followed.

Aside from the known fact that all three places had enslaved Blacks, one similarity among them was that the Blacks all suffered some form of mistreatment even after slavery was abolished in all three countries. In the United States of America, we learned that there were a lot of prejudices towards the Black people shown by the Whites. They treated the Black freed slaves badly. Similarly, in the Caribbean, Blacks were also ostracized after slavery was abolished. During the apprenticeship system, although the Blacks had a choice whether to work on the plantations where they were once used as slaves, they were forced to work under inhumane conditions when they opted to do so. The Blacks could be imprisoned for trivial reasons, and if they found themselves in prison, they would be flogged similarly to when they were slaves. Suriname also had an era where the Black ex-slaves, mainly the Maroons, were hunted like wild animals and killed. All these experiences show the common thread of some of the Blacks' abuse after slavery was abolished in The Unites States of America, the Caribbean, and Suriname.

Among the three regions, some of the laws affected Blacks. For example, they had limited representation in the laws causing their inability to vote. This impacted their ability to have their voices heard, as well as bring forth matters that affected them. That situation prompted the ex-slaves to protest the apprenticeship system and, as documented earlier in the literature, they demanded immediate, unconditional freedom. America was no better. We learned about the laws that were enacted by southern states called the Black Code.[134] These laws were used to keep Blacks under subjection as if they were still slaves. They may not have been slaves physically, but the laws promoted mental and emotional slavery. For example, some laws allowed only relative rights to Blacks. These Black codes prevented African Americans from "achieving political and economic autonomy."[135] Blacks could not testify in court against a White nor serve in the army. In the United States of America, it is said that tenant farmers had to sign labor contracts with White landowners annually. Failure to do so resulted in Blacks being arrested and hired out for work. Similarly, in the Caribbean, if slaves did not agree to work on the plantations full-time, they had to leave or pay rent to the Whites. If they did not do any of the above in the Caribbean, they would be evicted. This series of discriminatory laws of the state did not eradicate the concept of White supremacy. Suriname was no different as it relates to the laws being unjust.

Poor living conditions were also a common thread across all three regions after the abolition of slavery. In Suriname, such turmoil still exists to this day to the extent that currently, there is a refugee status attached to that state. During post-slavery in the United States of America, another grim situation the Blacks faced was having to live in severe poverty. They had very little sustenance and went through a lot of economic hardship. The Caribbean was not much different.

---

[134] Joel Williamson, *After Slavery: The Negro in South Carolina during Reconstruction, 1861-1877* (Chapel Hill, NC: University of North Carolina Press, 1965).
[135] Ibid.

Enslaved people received little compensation when they worked, and they were forbidden to work for more than one person.

Other noted similarities are the fact that Blacks in the Caribbean experienced a period among the Whites called a transition period, and those in Suriname also experienced something similar. The apprenticeship era saw the freed slaves working for eight years with pay, while the Blacks in Suriname had to work for ten years after slavery was abolished. The only slight difference was that the ten-year work period in Suriname was mandatory, while the eight-year work period in the Caribbean was not.[136]

After the slave trade ended and slavery was abolished, the planters in the Caribbean and Suriname alike wanted workers for their plantations. They did the same thing to obtain workers for their plantation. They started importing individuals known as indentured workers. Both the Caribbean and Suriname turned to similar places like China and India to seek workers. The indentured workers that came to the Caribbean were bonded to work for a certain amount of time. This time amounted to five years.

The United States of America, Suriname, and the Caribbean had persons who formed organized groups to protest the conditions that the Blacks had to endure during different periods. An example of this in America was the March on Washington that occurred on August 28, 1963. Civil rights leaders, which included Martin Luther King, Jr., joined forces to organize this march which they also attended. They assembled in Washington, D.C., to do a peaceful march, which aimed to force civil rights legislation and establish job equality for everyone.[137]

Although slavery was abolished, all these territories were ruled by the Europeans that colonized them. As we can recall, these colonial rulers made laws

---

[136] Jacqueline Jones and M. H. Jung, "Outlawing 'Coolies': Race, Nation, and Empire in the Age of Emancipation," in *The Best American History Essays 2007* (Palgrave Macmillan, 2007), pp. 111-133.

[137] Andrea Fetchik, *The American Civil Rights Movement* (ACLS Humanities E-Book, 2019).

that oppressed the slaves; however, there was very little that the slaves could do about it. They were forced to conform to these laws or otherwise suffer adverse consequences. Suriname, The United States of America, and different islands in the Caribbean eventually gained their independence from these colonial masters. Islands such as Jamaica, which became independent on August 6, 1962, and Trinidad, which gained their independence shortly thereafter on August 31, 1962, were free to set up their own governmental rule. They could now craft their own constitution, as well as create laws that were more in favor of the Blacks. Suriname also gained its independence on November 25, 1975.[138]

Another similarity we see is that all countries of note took the initiative to set up their own government systems, and Blacks started to claim their own space in the decision-making process. We read about examples of this in the United States of America. African Americans continued to be elected to different government offices. For example, Douglas Wilder was elected as the first African American governor in 1990, and Barack Obama was elected as the 44th President of the United States of America on November 4, 2008.[139] On November 3, 2020, Kamala Harris became the first woman and the first woman of color to be elected vice-president, the nation's second-highest office, in the United States of America. The United States Congress is also reported to have a large proportion of African American representation.

---

[138] Central Intelligence Agency, *The World Factbook 2016-17*, 50th ed. (Washington, D.C.: Central Intelligence Agency, 2016).

[139] Andrew Glass, "Barack Obama Elected 44th U.S. President, Nov. 4, 2008," POLITICO, November 4, 2011, https://www.politico.com/story/2013/11/barack-obama-elected-44th-us-president-nov-4-2008-099280.

CHAPTER 8

FORT BUKU AND THE CORDON PATH

MALOGASSI

"A betee mi buku, da mi dede"

(I would rather turn into dust than die)

[Ndyuka Proverb]

D uring Dutch colonial rule, Bokilifu Boni (famous as Boni) (ca. 1730 – February 19, 1793) was a guerrilla leader and freedom fighter in Suriname. He was born in Cottica to an African mother who was enslaved to a Dutch master and escaped afterward.[140] He grew up in the forest with her, among the Maroons. His supporters became known as Boni's people because he was such a strong leader (they become famously known as Aluku afterward).

They established a fort in the lowlands and raided Dutch crops along the coast. They crossed the river into French Guiana under the pressure of hundreds of freedmen and the Dutch regular army. From there, Boni continued to perform raids until he was killed in battle.

Boni's Life Story

My Ndyuka ancestors, history narrators, and some scholars said that Boni was a mixed-race person, born in freedom to a Dutchman and African slave. Boni's mother fled to the Cottica-Maroons' forest when she was pregnant. While pregnant, she ran into the woods to the Cottica-Maroons. Boni was born there in around 1730.[141]

---

[140] "Boni (Ca. 1730 – 1793), Leider Van De Slavenrevoltes in Suriname," IsGeschiedenis, October 9, 2020, https://isgeschiedenis.nl/nieuws/boni-ca-1730-1793-leider-van-de-slavenrevoltes-in-suriname#:~:text=Rond 1780 laaide de strijd, vermoord door Ndjuka-leider Bambi.

[141] Ibid.

His elders taught him fighting, fishing, and hunting. Boni was born in a tribe along the Cottica River in what is now known as the Town of Moengo in Suriname.[142]

In the 1760s, after the treaty signing with the Okanisi or Ndyuka people, on October 10, 1760, a young man named Bokilifu Boni arose, seen as the mightiest and most feared among the villages.[143] The most important thing about this Boni was that he was spiritually strong because of the religion and the knowledge from Africa that he possessed. No one could kill this Boni, and he did not want to have peace with the White man (Bakra). Consequently, when his group, the Okanisi eastern Maroons, signed the peace treaty, he refused to accept the treaty and comply.

The neighboring Ndyuka people signed a peace pact with the colonists in 1970, granting them territorial sovereignty.[144] Boni comes after Asikan Sylvester in 1765 as the leader of his tribe.[145] Boni aimed at a peace pact that was rejected by the Suriname society, followed by a war.[146] Negotiations were seen as a weakness mark by society.[147] The tribe consists of only 200 members, compared to 2,000 for the Ndyuka.[148] Lichtveld mentioned the Berbice slave rebellion as a potential

---

[142] Herman Daniël Benjamins en Joh. F. Snelleman and Joh. F. Snelleman, "Encyclopaedie van Nederlandsch West-Indië (1914-1917)," Dbnl, https://www.dbnl.org/.

[143] Wim Hoogbergen, "Origins of the Suriname Kwinti Maroons," *New West Indian Guide / Nieuwe West-Indische Gids* 66, no. 1-2 (January 1992): pp. 27-59, https://doi.org/10.1163/13822373-90002003.

[144] Martin Misiedjan, "The Ndyuka Treaty of 1760: A Conversation with Granman Gazon," Cultural Survival, December 1, 2001, https://www.culturalsurvival.org/publications/cultural-survival-quarterly/ndyuka-treaty-1760-conversation-granman-gazon.

[145] "Boni (Ca. 1730 – 1793."

[146] Ibid.

[147] Ben Scholtens, "Bosnegers En Overheid in Suriname: De Ontwikkeling van de Politieke Verhouding 1651-1992," New West Indian Guide / Nieuwe West-Indische Gids 70, no. 1/2 (1996): pp. 199–201.

[148] Ibid.

explanation for the policy change.[149] Whatever the inspiration, the first village was found and demolished in 1768.[150] Two more Maroon groups linked to the tribe in 1770 and become famous as "Boni's" (and Aluku afterward) after their leader's name. He trained his followers to become challenging opponents of the colonists. Joli-Coeur and Baron were his notorious fellow warriors.[151]

Fort Buku

Dutch colonial troops hunted the runaway Africans, who were also called the Bush Negroes or Maroons. These Maroons led a roaming existence because their villages were constantly being destroyed each time they settled, forcing them further into the jungle to build a refuge. In the second half of the 17th century, the runaway Africans built Buku (*bookoo*), an impregnable fortress. The story behind this fortress or stronghold is rooted in the story of one of the most renowned guerrilla leaders and freedom fighters in Suriname, Boni.[152]

Boni is the most popular slave hero leader in Suriname, and the story about Fort Buku has strong ties to his name. The story about the fortress he constructed is engrained in the history of Suriname when you hear about the Ndyuka people. Fort Buku was founded around 1770 by fled plantation slaves, Maroons, on an island in the middle of the swamps in the coastal area east of Paramaribo.

Boni and his warriors built Fort Buku around 1770 on an island in the middle of the swamps in the area of the Cottica River, and it was very hard to attack. According to history, this technique of building a fortress in the middle of a swamp

---

[149] Ibid.

[150] Céline Dobbeleir et al., "De Politieke Mobilisatie En Organisatie van Vijf Etnische Groepen in Suriname (PDF). Kennis Bank SU (in Dutch)" (University of Gent, n.d.), https://kennisbanksu.com/wp-content/uploads/2017/08/de-politieke-mobilisatie-en-organisatie-van-vijf-etnische-groepen-in-Suriname-Universiteit-van-Gent-Maele-Willems-Staete-Sarrazyn-Dobbeleir.pdf.

[151] Hans Buddingh, Geschiedenis van Suriname (in Dutch) (Het Spectrum, 1995).

[152] Wim S. M. Hoogbergen, The Boni Maroon Wars in Suriname (Leiden: BRILL, 1990).

was used before by other Maroons. This massive fortress was made completely out of wood. The outside wall was made of thick wooden palisades and was four meters high.

It was named after the Buku Creek and was situated in the wetlands of Commewijne's coastal area,[153] east of the Barbakoeba Kreek (Barbakoeba Creek) and north of the Cassipera. They chose the name Buku which means "dilapidated," and signifies the Maroons' motto, which sent the message based on its name that they *"would rather die than surrender and return to becoming slaves again, or I rather turn to dust.*[154] "This was because the penalty for a Maroon who escaped and was caught was death by burning. These creeks flow through a wetland that is intersected by sand or shaved prongs. The fortified village was on a sand zipper in a deep swamp called the Birbiri. Fort Buku was difficult to find and approach. The Maroons who knew the area well could attack plantations on foot or by canoe and return with their loot while it was difficult for pursuers to find them. It is believed that Buku was a mysterious creek. Up to this day, it is still seen as very mysterious. It is a sacred place for the Maroons at the Cottica River.[155] As a child, I remember that we were asked to be silent every time we would pass near the Buku creek as a sign of reverence to our ancestors, who sacrificed their lives to save fellow Africans. The wetlands provided strategic protection, and a cannon and rifles were used by them to arm the garrison.[156]

---

[153] Pieter Van Maele , "Op Zoek Naar Fort Boekoe," Trouw, September 7, 2012, https://www.trouw.nl/nieuws/op-zoek-naar-fort-boekoe~bfd676d4/?referrer=https3A2F2Fwww.google.com2F.

[154] Hoogbergen, "The Boni Maroon Wars."

[155] In 1997 and 2002 attempts were made to find the location and possible remnants of Fort Buku. During a third expedition in 2004, the researchers found an increase in a swamp corresponding to old travel reports. Metal remains, pottery and glass fragments were also found near this site. A checkup in 2011 by an archaeologist from Leiden University however, did not provide conclusive evidence that the remains of former habitation found came from Fort Buku.

[156] "Boni (Ca. 1730 – 1793."

It became challenging for the Dutch militia to trace them. Such a strong position enabled the Boni to raid the plantations on Suriname's east, particularly in the Cottica river region, several times. They took supplies, equipment, guns, and women during these raids. The victories of Boni's troops encouraged slaves to flee and join their group.[157]

Fort Buku was regarded as a relatively large island with villages, and it was used as army barracks and a refuge against the Dutch colonial army attacks. The swamp surrounding Fort Buku was deep, and an adult-sized male would stand in chest-high water in the swamp. Fort Buku was Boni's command post, and from there, he would launch his attacks on the plantations. The ammunition that he used was also kept at Fort Buku. These ammunitions included guns, pistols, and cannons.

---

[157] Ibid.

March thro' a swamp or Marsh in Terra-firma.

Figure 65 Dutch Colonial Soldier Attacks Fort Buku

The only way to have safely reached Fort Buku was via a secret path that was created underwater. This was deliberately constructed underwater, and it was not visible from ashore. In addition to this secret entrance, Boni also constructed some dummy paths that ended in the middle of the swamp. The colonial army's first attempt at capturing Fort Buku ended in an embarrassing defeat for the Dutch colonials. Boni captured those soldiers who could not get away and executed them.

The loss of slaves represented a significant loss of money for the planters. The fortress had become a key problem for the colonists due to the attacks and raids carried out from Buku and the costly punishing expeditions that proceeded. Boni's guerilla tactics were difficult to handle for the colony's militia.

The defeat of the colonial soldiers prompted the Dutch colonial government to change attack strategies. They realized the fort was surrounded by treacherous marshes, and the Maroons had equipped themselves with guns and a cannon as well as the location; the fort was almost impossible to find and unreachable for the soldiers of the Colonial Authority, creating the need to employ a new tactic.

Figure 66 Sketch of Fort Buku

In 1772, a corps of Zwarte Jagers (translation: black hunters), also known as the Black Rangers, was created from 300 freed slaves that European officers commanded to complement the militia.[158] If those slaves were enrolled as soldiers, they were granted freedom as well as a plot of land. They wore red caps to differentiate themselves from Boni's soldiers and became famous as the

---

[158] Ibid.

pseudonym Redi Musus (*rih dee moo soos*).[159] It is to note that "Redi Musu" to this day is an insult as it means traitor.

After a seven-month secret campaign, their crops became successful. This campaign included a secret path that gave access to the fort. However, this path underwater was exposed in 1772. The Jagers used the secret way to attack the fort when Captain Mangold made a feint assault. The fort was ruined, but Boni somehow fled to the east, crossing the Marowijne River on the French Guiana border.[160]

He relocated his headquarters to Fort Aluku. Further troops came from the Dutch Republic in February 1773. The troops were the marine regiment under the supervision of Colonel Louis Henri Fourgeoud. John Gabriel Stedman, who wrote a book about his experiences, was among the officers.[161] In his book, he explained how Boni used fierce guerilla tactics such as using four or five men to move and shoot rapidly to deceive and give the impression that there was an extensive group. Boni and his mobile warriors baffled the Europeans and their mercenaries by recognizing the wetlands and territories and defeated them several times.[162]

---

[159] Maele, "Op Zoek Naar Fort Boekoe."

[160] "Boni (Ca. 1730 – 1793)."

[161] John Gabriel Stedman, William Blake, and Francesco Bartolozzi, *Narrative, of a Five Years' Expedition, against the Revolted Negroes of Surinam, in Guiana, on the Wild Coast of South America, from the Year 1772, to 1777: Elucidating the History of That Country and Describing Its Productions ... with an Account of the Indians of Guiana, & Negroes of Guinea* (London: Printed for J. Johnson ... & J. Edwards, 1796).

[162] Silvia Wilhelmina Groot, "Rebellie Der Zwarte Jagers: De Nasleep Van De Bonni-Oorlogen 1788-1809," *The Guide*, 1970, https://dbnl.nl/tekst/_gid001197001_01/_gid001197001_01_0083.php?q=Rebellie der Zwarte Jagers. De nasleep van de Bonni-oorlogen.

Boni Established Fort Aluku

They eventually withdrew into French Guiana.[163] In 1777, the French intendant Pierre Victor Malouet went to Paramaribo to meet the Dutch representatives to discuss the 200 Maroons on French soil.[164]

The remaining Boni's moved to the south and settled at Suriname and French Guiana's border along a river known as the Lawa River.[165] They were initially attacked by the Ndyuka for invading their territory. After months of discussions, the two tribes concluded a peace accord in late 1779.[166] A Ndyuka Gaanman's daughter was offered to Boni as a wife.[167] Colonists got disturbed by the treaty, but the Ndyuka told them that Boni had promised not to invade the plantations if his people were not bothered.[168] Until 1788, when the plantation, Clarenbeek, was attacked, peace resided. After killing five soldiers, the plantation owner was kidnapped and forced to work for the tribe as a slave.[169] The Ndyukas joined the colonists after ending the peace treaty in 1789.[170] After the conquer of Fort Aluku in the next year, the plantation owner was freed from slavery.[171]

Bokilifu Boni was very angry with the system that enslaved his brother and his sisters. He said he would never stop until he killed all the White people that enslaved them. This was a problem in the interior of the Okanisi group, for their leaders had signed a peace treaty agreeing not to attack the plantations, but Boni,

---

[163] Ibid.

[164] Bernard Coppens , "Pierre Victor Malouet," 1789-1815, 2006, http://www.1789-1815.com/p_malouet.htm.

[165] "Boni (Ca.1730 - 1793)."

[166] Groot, "Rebellie Der Zwarte Jagers."

[167] Marie Fleury, "Gaan Mawina, Le Marouini (Haut Maroni) Au Cœur De l'Histoire Des Noirs Marrons Boni/Aluku Et Des Amérindiens Wayana1," *Revue d'Ethnoécologie*, no. 13 (February 2018), https://doi.org/10.4000/ethnoecologie.3534.

[168] Groot, "Rebellie Der Zwarte Jagers."

[169] Ibid.

[170] "Boni (Ca. 1730 – 1793)."

[171] Groot, "Rebellie Der Zwarte Jagers."

who was from the Aluku tribe, violated the treaty.[172] Boni did not want to see any White person alive. Treaty or no treaty, he felt they should all die for the atrocities they had inflicted on his brothers and sisters from Africa. Boni was later killed by being stripped of his strength, like in the Bible story of Sampson and Delilah.

The Plot to Kill Boni, The Seduction of Obia

Oral and Written Story

The Ndyuka tribe waged war against the Aluku tribe. Since Boni was violating the peace treaty, the Ndyukas vowed to kill him. This oral story is very sacred among the six maroon tribes in Suriname. Boni was feared by the Ndyukas, along with the other tribes. He operated under the influence of supernatural powers, making him almost untouchable. There was one woman, a medium named Ma Susana, who was married to Da Ainge, a Ndyuka man. She was an extraordinary woman, a real obia woman who went by the name Nengeekondee Mama. When the Ndyuka people use the word nengeekondee, it describes a high form of obia. Ma Susana heard about the situation and promised her husband, Da Ainge, that she would take on Boni and kill him. She had an obia upon her by the name Ma Mutombe. For her upcoming mission, she would have to take a lot of time to prepare this obia. When she finished this obia, she let the obia fly away like a pigeon. According to the story, the dove took possession of a *tei ondoo kamisa*, a loincloth worn by Boni. Ma-Susana performed her obia on his kamisa and it turned into a monkey. The monkey traveled through the forest to the Aluku. On arrival, the monkey stole the tool (obia) from Boni and returned it to the Ndyukas. Thanks to the work that Ma Susana performed with the obia of Boni, the monkey turned into a beautiful woman. Boni's sister saw him with the woman and warned him not to associate himself with that woman because she received a warning from the obia. Boni ignored his sister. "How can I not lust after such a beautiful woman?"

---

[172] Silvia W. de Groot, "Maroon Women as Ancestors, Priests and Mediums in Surinam," *Slavery & Abolition* 7, no. 2 (1986): pp. 160-174, https://doi.org/10.1080/01440398608574910.

he asked her. He had a weakness for beautiful women and took this woman in as one of his wives. The woman urged Boni to give her his *kina* (secret). Boni did not know that he did not have a real woman before him but an obia. The woman soon became impregnated by him and gave birth to a baby. She would sometimes braid Boni's hair and kept trying to get Boni's secret. On many occasions, Boni became irritated and would ask, "Why are you asking me these things?" While this woman quietly anticipated a response from Boni, one time he said, "One of my secrets is that bullets of lead cannot kill me *(loto á poi kii mi)*." This is a common expression of obia men. "The only bullet that can penetrate my body is when you melt a hammer that is used to nail coffins and mold it into a bullet that fits in a rifle." When he revealed this secret to the woman, at that same time, the board of the whole house groaned with a deep sound. It was the obia warning Boni, but he paid him no attention. The woman continued to talk to Boni and ask about all his secrets. He finally revealed another secret. He said under no circumstances should he come in contact with newborn children because the moment he touches one, he would lose his power.

After he revealed the second secret to the woman, Boni's obia was startled by how careless he was being. There was an even greater sound of moaning coming from the shelves of his house. Shortly after that, it was evident that Boni had to pay for his carelessness because the woman who had a newborn baby in her lap threw the baby in Boni's lap and disappeared. Boni was devastated. "Now it has happened to me!" he screamed. "Now it has happened to me! My enemy can now defeat me!"

Now that they had Boni's secret, he was vulnerable and susceptible to the attack of the Ndyuka. On February 19, 1793, Boni set up camp near the rapids with a name similar to the Marouini River, famous as Akuba Booko Goo (English: Akuba's Broken Gourd).[173] That night was the night of Boni's defeat. He was killed

---

[173] Fleury, "Gaan Mawina."

under the leadership of Ndyuka chief, Bambi.[174] Bambi did this by getting pressured by Lieutenant Stoelman, commander of the Redi Musus. The Ndyuka prepared for war against Boni, and one of the members of the Ndyuka clan named Da Baai prepared the bullet in his obia *osu* (house). Meanwhile, Boni and his people fled and looked for safety since he knew that the Ndyuka would be coming for him. After he ran for safety, he was caught, and they shot bullets at him, but none of the bullets hurt him. The bullet that hit him and finally struck his heart was the bullet that was manufactured under Ma Susana's direction. Some elders within the Ndyuka community believe that the bullet was fired by either Da Kwadidjo Ainge or Kwamala Baai. He was stone dead but did not fall. He remained upright. Many of those obia men tried to knock him down, but they could not. The same Da Baai who prepared the bullet was able to knock him down, and he was decapitated. After Boni was killed and decapitated, the Ndyukas took his head to the *bakaa (White man)*. The canoe that was transporting the head overturned in the *sama ede sula* (waterfall), and Boni's head was lost but was later recovered by the bakaa.

Lieutenant Colonel Beutler followed the Boni out of Suriname and into French Guiana in 1791.[175] The Suriname community still considers Boni a legend. Maroons in Suriname fought for their independence rights from 1887 till the peace agreement by the Kwinti.[176]

Adjako Basiton Benti

There was another story of a man who could read and write at the time of the peace treaty when both the Saamakas and the Ndyukas were undergoing treaty

---

[174] "Boni (Ca. 1730 – 1793)."

[175] Ibid.

[176] Hoogbergen, "Origins of the Suriname Kwinti Maroons."

negotiations with the Whites. This man's name was Adjako Basiton Benti.[177] "Basiton" means Boston, and "Benti" is Bent.

He was a slave in Jamaica, and the slave master that he was with taught him how to read, providing him with the ability to both read and write. His slave master, however, went out of business, severed ties with Jamaica, and went back to England, thus selling Basiton to the Dutch company in Suriname that was doing business - slave business with every country. Basiton Benti then proceeded to flee to Suriname and escape slavery. Contrary to his original plan, Basiton did experience slavery in Suriname. However, he was able to flee slavery almost immediately after he arrived in Suriname. He became the designated one to write the peace treaty and review the written contents of the treaty with the White man. Furthermore, Basiton had more articles in his treaty than the treaty that was signed before with the Saamaka people because he could read and identify the treaty's flaws.[178] This new, revised treaty still had flaws, but it was a better treaty than the first draft. Basiton turned out to be one of the strongest advocates of creating peace among the Maroons and Whites. There was a story going around that a Jamaican Maroon came to Suriname to help the other Maroons to freedom, but that was not a true depiction of the occurrences that were taking place. Basiton was not a Jamaican when he came to Suriname, but rather he resided in Jamaica as a slave. It was only when he came to Suriname that he was deemed as a Maroon, belonging to my grandfather's clan. I believe I still have his way of fighting for freedom, negating the contemporary way of enslavement, with the knowledge and resilience thinking that one should strive to have and create a better life. There are some struggles still going on in Maroon villages, as the Maroons are the

---

[177] C.N. Dubelaar and André Pakosie, "Kago Buku : Notes by Captain Kago from Tabiki Tapahoni River, Suriname, Written in Afaka Script," *New West Indian Guide / Nieuwe West-Indische Gids* 67, no. 3-4 (January 1993): pp. 239-279, https://doi.org/10.1163/13822373-90002667.

[178] Van der Linden, Marcel. "The Okanisi: A Surinamese Maroon Community, C.1712–2010." *International Review of Social History* 60, no. 3 (2015): 463–90. doi:10.1017/S0020859015000383.

poorest in the nation. The Maroons and the Amerindians are the poorest in Suriname, relatively.[179] We use the term, relatively, because we now have the opportunity for many Maroons to attend school and obtain a formal education.

Modern Day Fort Buku

Until today, Buku has an important symbolic significance in the history of slave resistance in Suriname. Military barracks in the capital, Paramaribo, are named after that fort: Membre Buku, which means "Remember Fort Buku." Fort Buku, as we know, was legendary for its location in the impassable swamp around the Cottica River until it was traced by the colonial rulers in 1772 and destroyed. In 2004, John Pel was convinced that he had found the place again, but that certainty continues to diminish because archeologists have made several trips there and could not find the exact spot. During archaeological expeditions, the trip was still not without risk.

The Buku kreek (Buku Creek) is navigable with some effort at the mouth of the river, but behind the forest, in the swamp where the creek originates, the vegetation becomes treacherous. On one of the islands east of the Buku kreek origin, surrounded by a deep swamp to the north and south, but approachable via a sand and shell zipper in the northwest, the legendary Buku Fort must have once been situated.

A group of Dutchmen, led by explorer, John Pel, after various fruitless expeditions, finally rediscovered the fort in April 2004. At least, a place was found that met the descriptions and maps made by the colonial army in the 18th century. What initially started as the dream of a few adventurers was adopted by the Scientific Information Foundation (SIF) in Paramaribo. In the meantime, Menno Hoogland, professor of Caribbean archeology at the University of Leiden, was called in to give a definitive answer about the exact location. With new source

---

[179] Jack Menke, et al., "The Political Culture of Democracy in Suriname and in the Americas, 2012: Towards Equality of Opportunity, 2013," *USAID from the American People*, June 2013.

material, the history of the Boni wars, and with it a piece of Surinamese history, can be rewritten from a non-Eurocentric perspective.

Figure 67 Picture of What They Believe to be the Swamp that Surrounded the Ancient Fort Buku

During the many trips that Pel made in recent years, he reported that he had to navigate the swamp in the same way Boni and the other Maroons did. To access this area, there had to be regular plowing through the thick vegetation. It is said that the terrain is constantly changing. One moment the grass is at your waist; a while later, it grows far above your head. In the dry season, it is necessary to cut the grass down considerably to find the bed of the creek through the vegetation. After a very wet period, the water gets so high that there is no difference between the creek and the swamp.

The inhospitable area does not seem suitable for living. However, in those centuries, when the Maroons inhabited the area, they had very little choice. A large number of them had fled the heavy plantation life and moved into the area after French sailor, Cassard, carried out an attack on the plantations along the Cottica and Commewijne River in 1712. The enslaved were sent into the forest by the plantation owners, confident that a large part would return. The most fertile parts of the area were already inhabited by the Aucan people.

Even though the archaeologist was able to do his job well, the expedition did not deliver the desired results. "No, we have not been able to prove that Fort Buku was actually here," Pel admits. Even more indirect indications were found, such as remnants of agricultural plots and small metal remains on the sand zipper. Wood residues from the palisades proved to be untraceable. "The evidence is poor. We have not found anything on the island itself." New historical source research must show whether or not something has gone wrong. But Pel remains determined, "I am open to alternatives, but until then, I believe it must be here." So, for the time being, the legend of Fort Buku still exists. What if we as Ndyuka people know where Fort Buku is but do not want to give that away because it is sacred to us?

What if we know, and with "we," I mean Ndyuka people from that region? What if we know where Buku is, and we do not want to release that information? Since the days of Boni, who built this impregnable fort, this place was considered a sacred place that protected the runaway Africans, and it is still considered sacred today by the Ndyuka people. That is the place where they conquered the colonial soldiers multiple times, and it was recorded in world history. It is a place that they take pride in and have it as a testimony of the physical and spiritual power they possessed after the colonial soldiers conquered the fort with the help of Ndyuka traitors. Since Fort Buku was destroyed in the 1700s, there has been a search for its location. For the past 20 years, expedition groups consisting of researchers and archeologists sponsored by the Dutch royal kingdom have tried multiple times to find Fort Buku through existing maps or through maps that were drawn by colonial soldiers. Every time they went to the Cottica area, with the help of locals, they tried to get to the fort with the help of locals, and it has been unsuccessful until now. At one point, they confirmed that they had found it, but to their disappointment, they realized that they had not. From what we know, based on the Ndyuka tradition, Fort Buku should remain hidden from everybody that they consider outsiders and who do not uphold their Ndyuka tradition, namely Whites.

Figure 68 The Swamp Where Fort Buku was Established Close to the Buku Creek

The truth is that elders who were given charge by our ancestors know exactly where this place is. For them, guiding individuals they do not think are supposed to be there would be a betrayal of their ancestors. Their own Ndyuka people had betrayed them by leading White colonial soldiers over to destroy the fort, to then lead White researchers to the ruins they now consider sacred would be considered a double betrayal. The designated elders are fully aware of that, and they will make sure that history never repeats itself.

The Cordon Path: Why Was It Constructed and by Whom?

The Amerindians and Africans still maintained their territories, creating routes within these territories to raid plantations and execute an escape. Consequently, a path was created to border the territory. The path is 94 km/58.4 miles long and 10 meters/32.9 feet wide. It starts behind Jodensavanne in the district of Para and runs almost to the Cottica River in the Marowijne district. This path was called the

Cordonpad (Cordon path).[180] The colonial government had to set up a cordon of guard posts in connection with state security. The word cordon derives from the French word *cordon,* which means line and indicated a line of armed posts in a military sense. The "Cordon Path" was ordered to be constructed in 1774 by Governor Nepveu for military defense." In 1776, it was legally established that the Cordon path should be built. The government was therefore compelled to cope with the attacks on the scattered plantations. In 1778, the path was completed. They made a path that would separate the villages from the colonial plantations. This pad is still there to view; it is next to my father's village called "Wan Hati," meaning *"One Heart."* When the free Africans would cross over to the other side to where the government had authority, and they got caught, then such a person would be enslaved again. If one did not cross it, they would remain in freedom.[181] It was like the path divided Suriname into two halves. The good news for the enslaved and free Africans was that the Cordon Path was long and wide and was very expensive to maintain. Therefore, the colonial government was unable to maintain the guard posts.

This path was made because it was thought that the path would protect the plantations in the eastern part of Suriname against attacks from rebellious Maroons, and at the same time, the Cordon Path would discourage slaves from running away. The Cordon Path served to prevent slaves from fleeing from the north to the free south and to prevent refugees from stealing from the plantations in the north.

---

[180] Humphrey Lamur, "The Impact of Maroon Wars on Population Policy during Slavery in Suriname," Journal of Caribbean History 23, no. 1 (1989): pp. 1-27.

[181] Hoogbergen, "The History of the Suriname Maroons."

Figure 69 Photo of the Cordon Path

Both sides of the path had gutters with a depth of 1.20 meters. Starting at the military Post Gelderland near Jodensavanne, the path led to Post Vredenburgh at Oranje Creek, near the coast. Every five kilometers, a watch post was built. More than 1,100 soldiers were populating the trail of the Cordon Path at the time. It is said that there was a military line with military posts that formed a cordon along the Cordon Path. There were 5 captains, 19 lieutenants, 44 sergeants, 69 corporals, 24 orderlies, medics, and 5 bakers. It is believed that there was a total of 955 men enlisted there.

Along the Cordon Path, there were obstacles placed there intended to slow down or prevent the slaves from either leaving the plantations to join Maroon fortresses or stopping escaped slaves from infiltrating the plantations. They planted shrubs as hedges that measured about four to five feet tall. These shrubs had thorns on them (commonly called Macka) which were hazardous to anyone who encountered the plants. They also littered the path with broken bottles and glass. This defense strategy against the slaves was thought to be effective by those who built this path because the slaves used to walk barefooted. Upon encounter with these hazardous barriers, slaves would suffer severe damage. Two soldiers constantly inspected the path to ensure that there were no holes there and that its reliability remained intact.

The military posts were reinforced in case an alarm was sounded. Every military post along the Cordon Path had a military drummer for reveille and retreat. These military drummers used to sound the alarm and sound the drums by using prearranged codes. Each of the military posts along the Cordon Path had a horse that messengers used to deliver urgent messages from post to post. The rule was that each horse only traveled for half an hour so that each post would have a fresh horse to use.

How did the Cordon Path Benefit the Ndyuka People?

Before the military posts were officially constructed along the path eventually named the Cordon Path, the Maroons used the path as an escape route to travel to freedom on the eastern side of the plantations. Most of the work on the plantations was done by African slaves who were not treated very well, and in the Caribbean region, Suriname had a bad name concerning slave treatment. Because of the treatment that the slaves received, many of them fled into the jungle. The geography of Suriname favored the escaped slaves since the plantations were near swamps, rivers, and dense jungles. In addition, these areas were barely visible during the rainy season. It was indeed not too difficult for a slave to disappear unnoticed from a plantation, and they fled individually or in small groups into the forest. Therefore, the Cordon Path would be one of those areas that the Ndyuka people used as their escape route.

Based on information revealed in research materials, the path that eventually became known as the Cordon Path allowed for a route that could be used to attack the plantations. The Maroons would often raid the plantations to recruit new members and acquire women, weapons, food, and supplies. These attacks were often deadly for the planters and their families, and after several unsuccessful campaigns against the Maroons, the European authorities signed peace treaties in the 19th century, granting the Maroons sovereign status and trade rights.

CHAPTER 9

ANCIENT ORAL STORIES OR
THE NDYUKA MAROONS

"Ifii sokoo katuku yu o si mboma"
(If you disturb the python nest, you will see phyton)

Diitabiki is the official capital of the Ndyuka people. The Ndyuka people always had a fighting spirit, and with that same spirit, they left Africa. That fighting spirit built a strong resistance against oppression. As they fled from the plantation, in the very early days, they arrived at what they called Mama Ndyuka. They established camps and villages in that region of Mama Ndyuka, and they felt at home. They found it necessary to have the same leadership hierarchy that they used to have in Africa, with a king as chief, along with his assistants. They started that hierarchy in one of the villages they called *Bongo Doti. Bongo Doti* is where the first *Gaanman* or King of the Ndyuka, Fabi Labi Beyman, of the *Dikan-lo*, reigned for the first time over the Ndyuka people. Ndyuka people from other villages respected and accepted him as the first Gaanman. Fabi Labi is a Ghanaian name. When they went back to the interior, they took their African name. However, in more recent times, namely in the '60s and '70s, people would feel embarrassed to have these Maroon names as family names. After the death of Gaanman Fabi Labi Beyman, Diitabiki became the capital of the Ndyuka people and the residence of subsequent Gaanman from that moment forward. One of the main reasons Diitabiki became the capital is because, after the death of Gaanman Fabi Labi, there was a war among the Ndyuka people and the different lo as to who would become the next Gaanman. There was a different lo, which is the *Otoo-lo*, who won the battle and moved from Bongo Doti to Diitabiki. They installed their own Gaanman, and from that time on, Diitabiki was the residence of all the other Gaanman that followed. According to Da Kofi, the Chief Priest, Akontu Velanti became the Gaanman. Akontu Velanti was very influential amongst the Ndyuka people. He was knowledgeable, and many looked up to him for counsel and direction within the Ndyuka culture. He was also well-respected because of his knowledge of African culture and tradition. His influence extended beyond the Ndyuka people to the other Maroon tribes as well.

The name Diitabiki means "very valuable." It was valuable because of the great influence it had on other surrounding villages. To note, there has been a misinterpretation of the name Diitabiki. Many of the Surinamese people and state officials refer to it as *Drie Tabbetje* or *Dritabiki*. The word *dii* in the Okanisi language can mean the number three or expensive. In this case, it refers to being expensive or valuable. Another factor leading to its value was the fact that all the Gaanmen resided there, and all major rules and decisions related to Ndyuka laws were established there. Other Ndyuka villagers would make the pilgrimage annually to consult the Gaan Gadu 'Great God' oracle. Diitabiki, however, is no longer esteemed as the primary religious center.

Songs of Freedom

"Tamaa sonten miyaaw, tamaa sonten malowé"

(Tomorrow we will escape)

Slavery, as we have seen in various countries where slavery existed, had a representation of songs sung by slaves that were used as a communication code to share their plight for freedom. Even when they would leave the plantation, the self-emancipated Africans would bellow a song that the slave masters perceived as seemingly innocent. As the Africans appeared to entertain themselves, they would sing the lyrics, "*tamaa sonten miyaaw, tamaa sonten malowé,*" a song created during slavery times in the 16th and 17th centuries to secretly communicate a slave's plan to escape to their fellow Africans.

Day of the Maroon (*Lowe Man Dei*)

My Uncle André Pakosie was very instrumental in enlightening me on many of our ancestral stories when I was researching and writing this book. In one of our conversations, I asked him to elaborate on the origins and history of Maroon Day, and why it was so crucial for him to work and have this day recognized as a national day of celebration for the Maroon people in Suriname and throughout the world.

During our conversation, I learned that this initiative was started from the frustration he experienced as a young 13-year-old child. He longed to see the development of the Maroon community and witness both their ancestral struggle and freedom recognized and commemorated on a national level. As a young boy, he began to participate in meetings with village leaders. His vision and mission to advance the Maroons was met with opposition, but he did not allow these setbacks to detract him from his calling. The obstacles further fueled his resilience and perseverance, and he would not give up the fight for his people. One of Uncle André's initiatives in 1970 was a day to honor and remember the Maroon people. As head of Akifonga, a group of young people from Suriname's interior who advocated for the country's Maroon population, he had a unique vantage point in this situation.

From 1970 to 1974, Uncle André held discussions with various Maroon establishments, among them were various Lo interest groups. Maroon societal groups were also there to determine a day for a joint annual tribute and celebration of the historical freedom fight, to be recognized as the Day of the Maroons. He also discussed his idea with the four doenman (gaanmans): Gazon Matodja (Okanisi), 'Agbago' Jozef Daniël Aboikoni (Saamaka), Cornelis Zacharias Forster (Pamaka) and Alfred Aboné Lafanti (Matawai). A meeting with these senior Maroon officials took place in Paramaribo in 1973, in which they permitted Uncle André to proceed with his plan to execute the Day of the Maroons.

During this conference, Agbago Aboikoni, the eldest member of the Saamaka Maroons at that time, proposed that October 10th be commemorated as the day on which peace with the Okanisi was signed in 1760. He justified his suggestion by noting that the Okanisi Peace Treaty was the first peace treaty to be initiated.

It served as a precedent for the subsequent peace accords with the other Maroon clans. In response to the proposition made by Gaanman Agbago Aboikoni, the other stakeholders stood in agreement. Tata Tebini Anka, a well-known Saamaka historian at the time, then sang a traditional Saamaka independence song at the request of Gaanman Agbago Aboikoni. The four men then issued an official order to Uncle André, instructing him to investigate the precise date of the peace treaty with the Okanisi and to put into effect the institution of this day.

For years, Uncle André searched the Central Archives in Paramaribo in vain for the precise date on which the peace deal with the Okanisi was signed but was ultimately unsuccessful. At the time, the archives did not contain any information dating back to the years before 1845. In the end, Uncle André enlisted the help of Silvia W. de Groot, a historian at the University of Amsterdam, who was able to determine the year by consulting the State Archives in The Hague. Silvia de Groot notified Uncle André that in a letter dated August 19, 1973, the agreement with the Okanisi was noted effective on October 10, 1760.

Uncle André then met with the four individuals in July 1974 to examine the findings of his investigation. The following month, the results were presented at a general gathering of Akifonga at the Fatima Club in Paramaribo's 79 Calcuttastraat.

After a follow-up discussion with the individuals concerning the establishment of Maroons' Day, they further solidified their support for the project and made an audio recording of their agreement. Therefore, he was then granted full power and authority to continue establishing the Day of the Maroons. After a mass assembly in the Fatima Club building on September 16, 1974, Uncle André, as the organization's "General Secretary" (President), signed the agreement. This marked the official establishment of the Day of the Maroons.

The inaugural Maroon Day event took place on October 10, 1974, thanks to its formation committee, comprised of Uncle André as Chairman, Robert S. Asoiti as Vice-Chairman, and the following committee members: Mérida Dapaloe, Libi

Bribi, Petrus Bow, Waldo Abese, Eastersi Asoiti, Hendrik Saite, Charles Pedi, Ronald Adaba, Elco Kuwi, Senkwari Amok, Ajafoe Tolli, and Michel Kokoli.

On Thursday, October 10, 1974, at the Fatima club building in Paramaribo, the inaugural celebration of the Day of the Maroons launched. The number of people in attendance was staggering. Countless Maroons and Creoles assembled to partake of this momentous and historic occasion.

At the notable event, government officials Deputy Prime Minister and Minister of District Administration and Decentralization, Olton W. van Genderen, and the Minister of Education and Public Development, Dr. Ronald Venetiaan, also acting as one of Pakosie's advisors, were in attendance. Minister van Genderen and André RM Pakosie gave an official address to the public. Thereafter, a customary Sete Tafaa (reception) was thrown in honor of the guests.

Among the highlights of this inaugural commemoration of the Day of the Maroons was a show by the Akifonga cultural department, a demonstration by the Opo formation, and a performance by Bally Brashuis and his band, Blaka Buba. Uncle André's private archives inhabit a coveted recording of the event.

National Day

It has been an annual tradition in Suriname since 1974 to commemorate Maroon Day yearly on October 10th. Since 1983, the festival has also been held in K'iyo'kondee, a residential neighborhood of the Okanisi in Suriname's interior. K'iyo'kondee is a settlement on the Tapanahoni that the Okanisi established as the first community with formal 'Kondee' status.

Numerous letters were written to sequential governments after the initial celebration of Maroon Day in Suriname for land and title rights to be given to the Maroons and Indigenous population who dwelled there for over 300 years. Additionally, it was requested that October 10th be declared a national holiday. The pleas fell on deaf ears. While on three separate visits to Suriname (in January

2001, again in 2003, and in 2009), Uncle André, founder of the Day of the Maroons movement, brought this matter to President Venetian's notice yet another time.

President Ronald Venetiaan made a public commitment at the 2009 Maroons Day ceremony that the event would be observed as a Suriname national holiday. This is a significant acknowledgment of the liberation fight of the Maroon forefathers for the independence of Suriname. Following his election victory in 2010, the Bouterse administration officially formalized and recognized Maroon Day as a national holiday in Suriname. In 2010, after many years of struggle and with the assistance of other Maroons who shared his goal, Uncle André's dream was finally realized.

A similar initiative in the Netherlands was spearheaded by the Dufuni Foundation, with Etho With at the helm as chair. The Dufuni Foundation, led by Kensly G. Vrede, and other Maroon groups such as the Sabanapeti Foundation, Cottica Foundation, Wooko Makandie Foundation, Afaka, Zunta, and Seke Foundation, staged the Day of the Maroon each year in Utrecht on the first Saturday of October.

When the leaders of Suriname's five Maroon tribes visited the Netherlands in 1992, at the request of the then Committee on Support for the Development of the Interior (COOB), led by Uncle André, it was the most remarkable memorial in the country's history. The dignified leaders included Gaanman Gazon Matodja (Ndyuka), Gaanman Songo Aboikoni (Saamaka), Gaanman Oscar Lafanti (Matawai and Kwiinti) and Acting Gaanman Kamil Akilingie (Pamaka), in addition Kabiten Pishërë Ashiware, a leader of the Tiyo (Indigenous people of the interior of Suriname).

The Day of the Maroons was commemorated in the Netherlands in 2011 and 2012, thanks to the efforts of the councils of Kabiten and Basiya of the Okanisi, the Saamaka, and the Pamaka, in partnership with SAMON.

In 2007, when the Day of the Maroons was celebrated in the Netherlands, the previous Gaanman of the Saamaka, Belfon Aboikoni, was also in attendance to represent the Saamaka. The Day of the Maroons in the Netherlands is celebrated today by various groups in several locations, including Utrecht, Tilburg, Amsterdam, Rotterdam, and The Hague.

Since 2003, the Day of the Maroons has been observed on an annual basis in French Guiana. In 2012, celebrations commenced in Belgium, and the United States began to follow suit in 2015 moving forward.

Figure 70 This is Called 'boto ede (Front of a Canoo),' a Canoo that Points Towards the Sky and Symbolizes the Freedom of the Maroons

The Name Ndyuka

Where did the name Ndyuka come from? What is the meaning or definition of Ndyuka? Let us begin with the definition of Ndyuka. When you hear the name Ndyuka, you may think right away of the runaway Africans from slavery, or you might also think of the Maroons or what some people also refer to as the Bush Negroes in Suriname. Some people may also define them as warrior people and people who have or maintain a strong African tradition and culture that also goes along with the West African way of living and their spirituality. There has not been a clear definition of the name Ndyuka, other than the different stories or associations composed by writers on this subject. As a child of the land of the Ndyuka, coupled with my upbringing within the Ndyuka culture, and as being a scholar in higher education, I attempted to come up with a definition of the word Ndyuka that I believe may give us a definition that represents the Ndyuka in its totality. My definition of the word, Ndyuka, is the words I feel reflect the total embodiment of the Ndyuka people. Therefore, I present the definition of Ndyuka as:

1. Faith

Strong spirituality and belief in God and their ancestors.

2. Endurance

The fact or power of enduring an unpleasant or difficult process or situation without giving way.

3. Resilience

The capacity to recover quickly from difficulties and toughness.

4. Intelligence

The ability to acquire and apply knowledge and skills.

5. Intuitiveness

The power to discern the true nature of a person or situation.

There is an interesting story in our oral history about the origin of the name. Although the African people were enslaved, they always had a strong spiritual connection with their ancestors. They believed that their ancestors would always carry them on the unknown journey. They were fearless and determined to live as free people, and they demonstrated that with their fighting spirit against the oppression of the *bakaa*, the White plantation owners. According to Da Kofi/Jojo and many other storytellers, as the Africans fled from the plantation and into the jungle on their way through the thick, dense jungle, they headed towards the river, and on their way, they heard a bird chirping, *"Ndyuka, Ndyuka, Ndyuka."* As they approached closer to the river, the sound became clearer and clearer, *"Ndyuka, Ndyuka, Ndyuka."* These runaway Africans stopped and declared that their ancestors were speaking to them. It was not by accident that the bird was speaking, but the bird was sending a message that they should call themselves the Ndyuka. Since they did not have one set name for all the runaway Africans who were referred to as slaves on the plantations, the runaway Africans came into agreement that they should indeed adopt the name, Ndyuka, for those that fled to the eastern part of Suriname.

In recent years, there has been a different story that was told about the origin of the name, Ndyuka. It has been told that as these runaway Africans were fleeing, they were also heading towards the river. They finally reached the river, and the name of the river was *Mama Ndyuka Kiiki*, Mama Ndyuka Creek. As they reached this creek, they decided that they should adopt the name of the creek as the name of their tribe.

The Witch (Wisi)

What is *wisi*? Why is it that within the Okanisi culture, we cannot avoid this word? Wisi, in the Okanisi culture, may be described as a strong obsession of the Okanisi people. The Okanisi religion is the concept and idea that all men are constantly or continuously subject to the compulsion of evil. As an Okanisi, the word wisi is not unfamiliar to me. It is interesting to see the dynamics of wisi because, from an early age, I grew up among people, young and old, who were using this word frequently. This word was used so much that you could experience the obsessive effects of the wisi power. It was so commonly used that if someone did not like you or was jealous of you, they could label you as a witch *(wisiman)*. Being labeled as a wisiman meant that you posed some type of danger and people believed that you could physically and spiritually harm your fellow man. Therefore, they would avoid you at all costs, whether you were innocent or not. It appeared as though normal life among your village or Okanisi people was over as if there was some type of curse over your life. People would become afraid to associate themselves with you. I have seen how people's lives were ruined because they were labeled as a wisiman, and wisiman could be applied to a man or a woman.

In the Ndyuka culture, nobody dies because of natural causes. It's amazing to see in my culture that it does not matter how old or how ill the person is; no one dies because of natural causes. For some reason, when someone passes away, in the Ndyuka culture, someone caused the individual to die. Some type of wisi, or wisiman, caused that person to die. It is hard to convince traditional Ndyukas that people can die of natural causes or due to an illness because in their mind, when someone passes away, it is due to the wisi of another, or ancestral spirits must have killed that person. Therefore, they have to call upon the gods and consult with them to find out who placed the spell on the person to cause death. Not to make light of the tradition and beliefs of my Ndyuka people, but in searching, consulting, and finding the person who caused the death, one would hope that they assess and find the right individual, but in my humble opinion, sometimes they did not get it right. Unfortunately, the wrongfully accused person would now be labeled as a wisiman for life until there arose a medium that attempted to implement a temporary solution to this situation. In the early 1970s, there was a self-proclaimed prophet by the name of Akalali Wootu, who claimed to be the support person of Tata Ogii, who used to be managed by Atyaimikule and Dominiki. This self-proclaimed prophet claimed that he was sent to re-establish order among the runaway and self-emancipated Africans. He referred to himself as the *Santigoon Futuboi*, which means a servant of Santigoon. According to him, there were too many injustices among the runaway people and the pandemic of witches that saturated villages for whom he was sent to eradicate. He also claimed that the spirit of the great god who was functioning in the Diitabiki area was upon him to bring reform. He provided rules as to how they should manage the operation and functionality of handling the deceased, the duration of time they should mourn the death of their loved ones, and the treatment of the witches.

He had a lot of followers because people admired him, but on the other hand, some people opposed his operation. As his popularity grew, he had to separate himself from his opposition; therefore, he established his own village called Nyun Kondee, and he was highly respected by the government back in Paramaribo. He was also given the title of Ede-Kabiten, Chief Captain.

Figure 71 Ede-kabiten, Chief Captain Akalali Wootu

His sole purpose and focus now turned towards his anti-witchcraft movement. People within the runaway society knew him as the anti-witch prophet. The whole notion of witches was out of hand. If someone was deceased and they were thought to be a witch, their corpse would be denied a proper burial. What would happen instead is that they would be buried on a piece of land in the jungle dedicated to witches. After the witches were deceased, they were taken by the pallbearers to this designated land, where they dumped their bodies and ran away as fast as they could. Their bodies were left there for wild animals and left open for decay because they were not worthy of a proper burial.

As a little boy, just like any other family would go to villages or camps or the countryside during holidays and school breaks, my siblings and I would go to the village. I remember being in the village with siblings and extended family and other kids from the village and those on vacation. It was a joyous time, making new friends with the other kids, where there were no televisions or cell phones to distract you, but a lot of fairy tales and Anansi stories. There were always older kids who knew a lot of stories and told us tales and jokes. Usually, their stories were reserved for the evening, while the days were reserved for all types of games. Among the storytelling, I remembered this story: the ritual of handling the dead witches of the village. You would be told that the pallbearer would take the witch, dump their casket, and dump their body in the jungle. As a little kid, you would just sit there thinking. The reality was that the village was surrounded by jungle. You start pondering, "Where in the world did they throw these people?" No one knew where this place was, other than the elders, and they would not tell the youth. Can you imagine the torture of going to sleep as a kid, because around midnight, the electricity would be turned off, and everything would become pitch black? Thus, at night, you would hope that they would tell you a good story, so you would not sit there worrying. The worry was even greater because there were some fruits you would have to go into the jungle and get. Some of the fruits were within short walking distance, but other fruits required you to walk a long distance to obtain them from the trees.

My mother used to use the term *Santigoon Futuboi* towards my uncle as a phrase that indicated a man of valor. This word or title signifies one with great strength. It is a terminology that is used often among the Okanisi as one that is a warrior and possesses great strength.

The Fire Ritual Site

The new anti-witch prophet, Santigoon Futuboi, set up his fire ritual site to drive the evil out. Outside of his new village, there was uninhabited land where he set up his burning site. People would come from different villages in great numbers to witness this ritual event. He called it a burning site to burn the witch (wisi). At the appointed time, the fire ritual would begin to cast evil out of the village. He would take the people suspected of witchcraft and command them one by one, to sit and undress down to their undergarments. He would then take a pangi (skirt) soaked in a secret mixture, set it on fire, and flare it above the suspected witch's bareback. Immense flames would shoot up high in the air. The accused could not keep their composure while the audience of over 200 villagers drew forward as another cloth was lit, eager to see if the remnants of the fiery flames of the pangi would land on the witch's bareback, an indication of their guilt. After the ritual, the accused were then deemed free of their sins and were allowed to return to their village.

If they were found guilty, there would be a ritual performed for them that included the drinking of libation. The drinking of libation was not necessarily something that they had to drink in large quantities, but you were required to sip the secret mixture of libation infused with human blood, feces, and other horrid ingredients. This mixture was a highly secretive mixture hidden from the public, yet this was the mixture that they would mix with their finger and put a tip of it on one's tongue to signify cleansing.

Many from the Ndyuka villages became Christians, and they did not believe in nor accept the anti-witch prophet, Akalali's, practices. In their opinion, Akalali's processes were targeted toward middle-aged and older women and men who were unattractive, poor, ill, or had some form of deformities. The Christians believed that Akalali did not have the power to set these people free from wisi, but only Jesus had the power to set anyone free. Akalali and his aids believed that these were the people who had reason to be jealous and seek vengeance on others. Towards the end of Akalali's practice, he believed that he had eradicated the witches in all the villages, so according to him, the villages were free from witches. On the contrary, many people, mostly well-to-do men, did not even go through his ritual screening process, which left reasonable doubt that there could have been several remaining witches unaccounted for. I saw him once as a kid, a man short in stature, but I, of course, had no business having any type of conversation with him. The truth is, the wisi and concept of wisi were not eradicated. To the present day, the Ndyuka people are still obsessed with wisi just as they were initially. There are still people who are being accused of being wisiman. The sad part is that even though some men are being accused, the majority (over 50%) of the accused are middle-aged and older women. Are women the only ones who are wisiman?

Ma Pansa

Rice *(alisi)*

African women brought rice from their homeland to Suriname in their hair. When they left Africa, they were intelligent enough to travel with rice (*alisi*). The women knew that food would be vital for life and sustainability, so as they braided their hair, they would secretly weave the rice grains into their cornrows, discreetly making provisions for their family in preparation for their unknown journey. One of the most popular women that brought rice from the plantation into the hidden forests of Suriname was Ma Pansa, mother of one of the largest Maroon tribes, the Saamaka tribe.

Many people from other countries such as the United States and New Zealand conducted tests on the Surinamese rice in the interior, and they were able to trace it back to Africa.

Cardamom

These runaway Africans managed not only to bring rice from Africa, but they managed to bring cardamom (*nenge konde pepe*) seeds in their hair to the plantation, and from the plantation, they brought it to the different villages. Even though cardamom was a spice to cook with, many within the Maroon community did not do much cooking with it. They regarded it as very sacred, and they used it mostly for medicinal purposes and even for ritual activities.

Figure 72 Cowrie Shells (Papa Moni)

Cowrie shell is very popular. Cowrie shell is not only popular, but it is also important within the African culture. Its use and meaning vary. It was used as money in Africa to do trade, and White Europeans used it to both purchase and pay slaves. In the early days of slavery, it was used for religious activities because of its value in rituals and used to decorate ornate statues for worship. It was also used in rituals to pay the gods. Therefore, one would not use this for any other purposes. It was considered very sacred. In more recent years, since it has not been used as money or a trade commodity, people began to use it more for jewelry. It took a while to bridge the gap from being used as money and religious sacrament to now using it as jewelry in our modern days. It also has other meanings, as it was viewed as a symbol of womanhood, power, wealth, and fertility.

Faya Siton

Songs of the fiery branding iron:
"Faya siton no brong me so,
no brong me so,
adjing masra Jan e kiri suma piking."
Firestone don't burn me so,
don't burn me so,
again, master Jan is killing somebody's child.

When I was a little boy, we sang this song a lot. We would also use a certain plant seed that looked similar to the eyes of a cow (*kow ai*). While singing, we would take this seed and rub it against a stone until it got hot. It would be so hot that if you put it against somebody's skin, it would burn them and peel the skin off. Now and then, we would do that to each other as kids. You can imagine the pain that we caused each other, but as we knew it then, it was just a song and a game we were playing. Little did we know that it had a deeper meaning than just playing and burning each other. In the early slave days in Suriname, slaves could not read or write. Therefore, they could not document the events happening on the plantations or in the villages. One way they documented events was through songs and oral stories. They made this song called *Faya Siton No Brong Me So* to document the pain they had to endure as the slave traders would brand their skin with a fiery branding iron. Every time they had to go through this process, it felt like they were dying; that is why they sang, again, master Jan (representing the White man) is killing somebody's child.

Beleey
"Luku so, na Beleey dyape, Luku so na Beleey dyape!
Heey na Beleey ooh!"
(Look, that's Beleey over there, Look, that's Beleey over there
Hey, that's Beleey ooh!)

These were the exciting words of all the passengers in the little canoe that was taking us to my mom's village. As they cried out saying that Beleey was on the bank of the creek, I saw Beleey on the bank of the creek with his kamisa on, and there was consternation in the boat of excitement. Of course, on one hand, I was also excited to see him, but on the other hand, I was more terrified of 1) the people remembering that we were in a small canoe that could flip at any moment, and 2) all the scary stories I heard of him in the village. Shortly after all the commotion, he did not hesitate at the river of the creek but dove head-first into the pitch-black river, and the curious people on the boat, including the canoe steerer, waited to see what would happen after Beleey had jumped in the water. I remember we stayed there for a long time, and until the time we left, we did not see him come back up. I was sitting there in the canoe in my youthful mind thinking, "What could have possibly happened to him?" Nothing happened to him, but this was his lifestyle. Long before we came to know the name "Aquaman," there was a real-life aqua man in Suriname, a man of water, or a human fish named Beleey/Belee. Beleey hailed from the village of Pikin Santi but lived in a village called Tamarin. Three of my sisters and one of my brothers knew him personally because they used to live in a Catholic boarding school founded by the Dutch in Tamarin.

Figure 73 The Real-Life Aqua Man Beleey

I heard different stories from my siblings about Beleey. My mom also knew him since he was a young man because my maternal grandpa Boideng is from the village Pikin Santi as well. It was said that Beleey did not stay on land long. From the time he was little until he was an old man, he spent most of his life either in the water or underwater. Beleey's parents, however, were not so active in the water. His mother was Pikin Eva, who he often referred to as Mama Tefa. He also had a younger sister named Saa Anolia, who was a great swimmer as well. She also spent most of her life in the water. Most people do not know much about her because the focus was more on Beleey.

There are several scenarios around the existence and the activities of Beleey in the Maroon community. Beleey was a unique individual. His fame and popularity were known among all Maroons and the six major Maroon tribes. Until today, his name, lifestyle, and activities are in regular everyday conversation among Maroons. The story of Beleey is not a fairytale; it is a real-life story, even though it may sound fictional. There are several scenarios surrounding his life that are factual events; however, it is unclear as to whether his acts stemmed from a supernatural power, natural God-given ability, or spirits from the gods. I was told that he could, based on the distance he was swimming, go as close to ten miles. Besides swimming far, he could stay for a long time underwater. It was inhuman for a person to be underwater for that long, sometimes almost half a day. Also, he would take his food with him underwater, and he would stay there and eat regularly. Another thing that is so mind-boggling is that in Suriname, we learn about geography in the 3rd grade, and one thing you learn about the Cottica River is that the Cottica River is not wide, but it is very deep. The Cottica River is not murky, but it is dark in color, so there is zero visibility. Beleey could dive and stay underneath the water, and even if somebody's object would fall in the water, all you would have to do is tell Beleey, and he would come back to shore with whatever that object was. Beleey was fearless, and that has raised a lot of questions within the Maroon community. For him to stay that long in the water at any given time, whether it was during the day or the night, he would not think twice before he jumped in the water. Every time he jumped in the water; he would stay for long periods before he came out. Understand the picture of how it was in the interior, there was no electricity, and the river was not lit. Coming outside at night was like you were facing a black wall. Between the river, sounds, and noises of the animals and all kinds of bush creatures, it would take you a good amount of courage to jump in that water, not knowing what was lurking beneath.

A lot of frustration and disappointment faced by many of the younger generations concerning Beleey's life was the fact that nobody in his time conducted research or did tests on him to figure out what his strengths were and what natural or spiritual ability caused him to be a little more than the average person. There are two accounts of his spiritual ability. The first account suggested that he may have had supernatural power from God above and that God had gifted him, so his gift to remain in water and underwater superseded the average human being. What the plan of God was with him, nobody knows, but the fact is that everybody knew it was not normal for him to stay that long in water and underwater. The second account among the Ndyuka was that he had contacted the wisi. It was said that because he did not go along with certain politics he disapproved of at that time, the people that were involved placed a spell on him in the form of a water spirit to keep him away from land. In other words, they wanted to make sure he stayed in the water for the rest of his life. If that is the case, then whoever placed that spell on him succeeded because he indeed never stayed on land. He even told some of my family members that a water spirit had spoken to him at the Coermotibo Creek (*Komotibo Kiiki*) and told him that he should not return to that creek, and he decided never to go back there. Many of the elders also confirmed that he did not possess a winti, an ancestral spirit that guided him. However, if he did have a winti, they were not aware of it, which would be uncommon for them not to recognize it. Still, the question remained, among the Maroons at large, whether he had a winti or not. The third account raised questions about his natural ability. By looking at him, people who had been around him described him as someone very fast and very humble. He was teased by the kids at the boarding school in his village because of the nasal tone of his voice. He also had a long torso and short legs, creating an unusual body frame. It is not scientifically proven that he had special lungs or had a way of expanding or compressing his lungs. It was also unclear whether he discovered some type of breathing object in the water that no one else knew, or maybe it was just his family genes that gave him the advantage of being so aquatic. Since he never got any type of testing, we cannot prove whether it was a natural ability or a God-given gift. Until then, these were some of his favorite words before he jumped into the water: "*A kaba now, Tjubung!*" (It is finished now, Splash!)

CHAPTER 10

NDYUKA INNOVATIONS AND HEROES

MALOGASSI

"Sabi fa fu du na mankee wi"

(There is no lack in knowhow among us)

There is one name that the Maroon people from Suriname will never forget, and that name is Kwasi. Ever since I was a little boy growing up in Suriname, I have always seen my parents using herbal remedies. In our household, they used herbal remedies for almost anything. If you had a headache or stomachache, they would give you something to drink. But there was one drink, in particular, with an extremely bitter taste that they would give you when you had a stomachache, virus, or inflammation. Also, for cleansing, whether it was the intestines or colon cleansing, they would give you this bitter tonic to drink. The good news is that after consumption, whatever ache, or pain you had would almost disappear immediately, and you could go back to play. It was a normal way of life to consume herbal remedies as Ndyuka people. This practice of herbal remedies did not start with my parents nor the Ndyuka people at large, but it started way back in Africa, also a regular practice of the enslaved Africans. One of the well-known remedies was discovered by an enslaved African named Kwasimukamba Tjedü-Tjedü. During the transatlantic slave trade, the Europeans had doctors on the slave ships and on the plantation, who would first inspect the slaves upon arrival on the ship and treat them for any illnesses as needed. Additionally, the Europeans faced scores of unmanageable diseases on the plantation, and they were desperately seeking ways to combat all the illnesses. Even though they took a lot of credit for most medical treatments discovered by Africans, there was one man named Kwasimukamba Tjedü-Tjedü, an African slave in Suriname who later earned his freedom of respect and recognition. He discovered a plant in the wild that cured diseases. This was an undisputed accomplishment that the Europeans could not deny, even though they were trying to take credit for it.

Figure 74 Gaanman Kwasimukamba Tjedü-Tjedü

Who was Kwasimukamba Tjedü-Tjedü? Kwasimukamba Tjedü-Tjedü was born in 1690 in Gold Coast, Ghana, West Africa. His name has many variations, such as Quacy, Kwasi, Kwesi, Quasi, and Quassi. Kwasi was an Akan Fanta, and his native name is Kwasimukanba Tjedü-Tjedü. He has many attributes to his name such as healer, freedman, planter, and spy. He assumed all these roles at one point in his life.[182]

Kwasimukamba Tjedü-Tjedü as a Healer. Why was Kwasimukamba Tjedü-Tjedü Called a Healer?

Kwasimukamba Tjedü-Tjedü was sold into slavery in Suriname to a Dutch slave trader in South America, and as a slave, he was also known as an obia man

---

[182] Kerry Lotzof, "Who Was Graman Kwasi?" Natural History Museum, accessed March 28, 2022, https://www.nhm.ac.uk/discover/who-was-graman-kwasi.html.

(one skilled in medical and spiritual knowledge). He used this to his advantage. Kwasimukamba Tjedü-Tjedü began to use his spiritual and medical knowledge to heal the Europeans and the slaves as well. As a slave, he was paid for his service, and with that, he became a very influential person. Kwasimukamba Tjedü-Tjedü was also a spy. Many people claimed that Kwasimukamba Tjedü-Tjedü reportedly became an informant for the Dutch and helped them capture many of the runaway Africans. The escaped Africans met the Amerindian people, who were the indigenous people. They looked for refuge amongst them.

As an informant, Kwasimukamba Tjedü-Tjedü worked for John Gabriel Stedman, a Scottish Dutch mercenary, to hunt down freedom fighters in Suriname. Lieutenant Stedman admired Kwasimukamba Tjedü-Tjedü so much that he named him Gaanman, which means "great man." This is a significant title to be called a Gaanman because later, after the abolishment of slavery where the Maroons founded 6 major tribes; they gave each of their kings the title of Gaanman, which is the highest office within the Maroon community.

This goes to show how highly regarded Kwasimukamba Tjedü-Tjedü was back in those days, not only by the European plantation owners but also by his fellow enslaved Africans. In essence, Kwasimukamba Tjedü-Tjedü was the first Gaanman. In 1777, after carefully observing Kwasimukamba Tjedü-Tjedü, Stedman wrote, "This African, by his insinuating temper and industry, not only obtained his freedom from a state of slavery but by his wonderful ingenuity and artful conduct found the means of procuring a very competent sustenance." Having got the name of a loekoman, or sorcerer, among the lower slaves, no crime of any consequence was committed, especially at the plantation, but Gaanman Kwasimukamba Tjedü-Tjedü, which signifies Great-man Kwasimukamba Tjedü-Tjedü, was instantly sent in to discover the perpetrators, which he very seldom missed. As a sorcerer, he occasionally received capital rewards for his services.[183] Within the Ndyuka community in Suriname, there are several oral stories and history about Kwasimukamba Tjedü-Tjedü. It was said that he used the secret weapon obtained from his ancestors to defeat the runaway Africans. Therefore, he was described as a traitor to whom the ancestors had bestowed their medical and spiritual knowledge. Tjedü-Tjedü used this medical and spiritual knowledge to lead the Europeans into their jungle to capture the runaway Africans.

The runaway Africans were furious with Kwasimukamba Tjedü-Tjedü, so much so that one of the chiefs cut off Kwasimukamba Tjedü-Tjedü's right ear.

One day, Kwasimukamba Tjedü-Tjedü gave word to the bakra (Whites) that he knew the way to Baakawata, one of the remote areas in which Saamakas lived. "Let me go all by myself," he said, "I'll lie to them, and then we can go and snatch them," and that is what he attempted to do. Kwasimukamba went alone. He claimed to have come to the Saamaka at Baakawata in the name of peace, not wanting to cause any trouble. He came and became their mati (close friend), and they dwelled together for a period. Now Kwasimukamba Tjedü-Tjedü took himself a wife from the Saamaka tribe. She was the sister of Ma Pansa, who was the wife of Chief Adoe Adjako, leader of the Saamaka tribe. When Kwasimukamba Tjedü-Tjedü arrived at Baakawata, Adoe Adjako embraced him like a mati. Kwasimukamba Tjedü-Tjedü would repeatedly ask Adoe Adjako to reveal the secret of his obia, that supernatural power that made him impenetrable. Adoe Adjako saw Kwasimukamba Tjedü-Tjedü as a confidant, until one day Wamba [an apüku (forest spirit) god who spoke through Adoe Adjako's sister, Jaja] warned him, "Beware, evil is on the way." After hearing of this possible betrayal of his brother, Adoe Adjako decided to deceive Kwasimukamba! He told him that his power lay within the small bunch of sugarcane growing in the back of his house.

---

[183] Richard Price, "Kwasimukamba's Gambit," *Bijdragen Tot De Taal-, Land- En Volkenkunde /Journal of the Humanities and Social Sciences of Southeast Asia* 135, no. 1 (1979): pp. 151-169, https://doi.org/10.1163/22134379-90002574.

Adoe Adjako said that if the sugarcane was shot at until it withered and dried up, he would die. One day, before the year had reached its end, Kwasimukamba Tjedü-Tjedü went down into the city, vanishing from the Saamakas. Little did they know that he went and piled soldiers into boats and led them up the river and near the Saamaka tribe for the attack. Then one early morning, at cock's crow, Wamba appeared, once again, to Jaja and crooned:

> *"Lukéin o, banangoma hesi é.*
> *Lukéin o, banangoma hesi o.*
> *Kwasimukamba tjai kibamba. [Repeat first 3 lines.]*
> *Banangoma hesi o."*

The spirit was saying, "They've come. That Kwasimukamba who disappeared is returning!" With this news, they hurried to consult the great obia pot, and to their dismay, it was boiling, indicating danger was present! That same day, the Whites arrived. They fled the village and disappeared into the corners of the forest as the Whites drew nearer. When the Whites arrived, Kwasimukamba Tjedü-Tjedü led them straight to the small stand of sugarcane. The Whites shot at the sugarcane for hours as if it were a target at a firing range! However, to their shock and disbelief, their fiery ambush was of no consequence because the sugarcane never withered. After watching this spectacle, Adjako re-emerged before the Whites with his cutlass and went straight to battle. He sliced and decapitated every single head except that of Kwasimukamba. Then Adjako said to him in fury, "Kwasimukamba Tjedü-Tjedü, when you were hungry, I fed you, and you ate until your belly was full. Now, look at the shame and disgrace you have become. I am not going to kill you, but I will make you a laughingstock in front of everyone." Adjako then snatched Kwasimukamba, stretched out his right ear with force, and chopped it clear off! Kwasimukamba, in anguish, said, "What hellish thing did you do to Kwasimukamba of Tjedü! When a person's ear is cut off, his face is ruined!" He then hurriedly left, in embarrassment and shame, for the city. Meanwhile, Kwasimukamba Tjedü-Tjedü's notoriety became more prevalent among the Europeans, and because of all his good deeds to the Europeans, they gave him a breastplate with the inscription, "Kwasimukamba Tjedü-Tjedü, faithful to the Whites." Kwasimukamba Tjedü-Tjedü was a faithful personal slave to the governor until he was free under the Manumission Act. As a member of the Ndyuka tribe, I must say that as much as I hated the way Kwasimukamba Tjedü-Tjedü conducted himself against his fellow Africans, admittedly, I am proud of his achievement in the natural sciences. Kwasimukamba Tjedü-Tjedü was accredited for being the first discoverer of Kwasi tonic or, as we know in our culture, the Kwasi bita (Kwasi bitter) drink. In 1730, the bitter wood was named after him. Scientifically known as Quassia amara (Amargo, Bitter-ash, Bitter-wood), it is a species in the genus Quassia.

Throughout Kwasimukamba Tjedü-Tjedü's life expansion, he attained great praise and rewards, on both a national and international scale, for his societal contributions. Additionally, his scientific genius was recognized by Carl Linnaeus, known as the father of modern taxonomy, who honorably named the plant Quassi amara (Kwasi bita), and Neils Dahlberg, a visiting Swedish naturalist who

Figure 75 Quassi Amara Cup

encountered Kwasimukamba Tjedü-Tjedü around 1761. Quassi amara is an organic nauseant (a substance that induces vomiting). The chemical, Quassin, extracted from the plant, is one of the world's most bitter elements. The plant serves as a therapeutic for fever, upset stomach, colon cleanser, or herbal tea. Additionally, its insecticidal agents prevent parasites, flea, and mosquito attacks.

Carl Linnaeus was privileged to have an up-close and personal view of this freedman, Kwasimukamba Tjedü-Tjedü, utilizing the amara plant to restore health and vitality to people by using the bitter tonic pulled from the plant. One notable difference in this advancement was that the Quassi plant did not induce diarrhea as a side effect, as seen with the Peruvian bark, a plant also commonly used and well-known for its medicinal properties. Quassia was proven to have no side effects, making it a major contender in the healing industry.[184]

Carl was fascinated with Kwasimukamba Tjedü-Tjedü's discovery, mainly because of the multiple medical gains accompanying these findings. As a result, Kwasimukamba Tjedü-Tjedü received full accreditation and acknowledgment for his plant discovery and medical innovations within the European landscape. On the contrary, Neils futilely attempted to assume ownership of Kwasimukamba Tjedü-Tjedü's work. Due to his European background, Neils deemed it an effortless feat to take credit for the discovery of an African named Kwasimukamba Tjedü-Tjedü. However, Neils left flabbergasted and dismayed, not obtaining his coveted accolades because he was not a true medical pioneer. In Europe, Kwasimukamba Tjedü-Tjedü's identity and notoriety accelerated beyond expectation. Furthermore, the proven safety and efficacy of his plant/product to help people caused Kwasimukamba Tjedü-Tjedü to be professionally accepted by the medical community and as a leader in Europe's pharmaceutical drug industry. Kwasi bita landed as one of the top medicinal remedies for various illnesses. To this day, Suriname continues to export Kwasi bita in mass quantities.

After the Surinamese people discovered the effectiveness of this plant, they started to use this plant in large quantities as a tradition and have exported large amounts of it to various parts of the world. Kwasimukamba Tjedü-Tjedü was deeply appreciated and honored for his service to the Europeans, namely by the

---

[184] "National History Museum," National History Museum London, https://www.nhm.ac.uk/.

Dutch in 1776. At that time, Kwasimukamba Tjedü-Tjedü was 80 years old when he met with the Prince of Orange in the Hague and was given full military regalia like that of the Dutch general.

After Kwasimukamba Tjedü-Tjedü left the kingdom of Orange in 1776, which is the Netherlands, he was highly favored and well-respected by the Dutch. He returned to Suriname, and this time, Kwasimukamba Tjedü-Tjedü, at 80 years old, had 3 different titles given to him to honor his work. One title given by the Dutch Monarch was General, the highest title in the Dutch Army, and he was also given the full military regalia of a Dutch General. Secondly, a General of the Dutch Army that used to be on the plantation gave him the title of Gaanman, accompanied by the breastplate that stated his loyalties to the Whites, namely the Europeans. Lastly, he was acknowledged and accepted by his fellow Africans and the Europeans as a bush doctor.[185] He was now a bonafide bush doctor. You can imagine he was no longer looked down upon as a Black African slave, and he was no longer looked down on as someone that could be recaptured and put back into slavery. He was no longer looked upon as a Black person who was a potential half breed between a White and an ape, according to earlier statements of some German researchers, and he was no longer looked upon as a strong African that was only good to do the harsh free labor on the plantation.

Consider what kind of influence Kwasimukamba had when he returned to Suriname. How the plantation owners viewed him, and how the captured African slaves viewed him. In the eyes of the Dutch army on the plantation, he was a General, established by the Kingdom of Orange and by the prince himself. The army and the plantation owner looked up to him with great respect because his ranking was higher than most of the military leaders; however, his fellow Africans met him with mixed feelings of both pride and betrayal, as they no longer saw him at the same level as them because, even though he received many accolades, they still considered him a traitor. They acknowledged his accomplishments, but they

---

[185] Ibid.

were not happy with the person he became. Although he was an African, he was regarded as White, and he no longer saw himself and his fellow Africans on the same level. Note that for Kwasimukamba Tjedü-Tjedü's fellow Africans, he was not only regarded as a General who was appointed by the Kingdom of Orange or as a Gaanman for showing his loyalty to the Dutch for being a traitor, but for the fellow Africans, it was very important that he was also a bush doctor. According to the African tradition, he was held to a higher standard because of African beliefs and traditions. With that, he did not give his fellow Africans much room to criticize him or to even harm him the way they would've liked to because he was considered a spiritual leader. Upon arrival in Suriname, he got one of the houses sponsored by the Dutch (grant housing), and during that time, he found his own plantation where he used his fellow Africans as slaves. Although Kwasimukamba Tjedü-Tjedü made significant earnings with his medicine, as one of the slave plantation owners, he accumulated wealth just like any other successful slave plantation. As with other successful slave plantations, he made himself rich by dirtying his hands in the slave business. Kwasimukamba Tjedü-Tjedü died as a very rich man.

Even though Kwasimukamba Tjedü-Tjedü is highly regarded within the different Maroon tribes in Suriname, some claim that he is from the Saamaka tribe because of the name Kwasimukamba Tjedü-Tjedü and because the oral story of him was narrated by some within the Saaramaka tribe. We know from history that Kwasimukamba Tjedü-Tjedü was not a Saamaka or could not have been a Saamaka because of what history is telling us. He was captured in Ghana and sold into slavery in Suriname, so his existence was before the establishment of the different tribes, which happened after the abolition of slavery.

Jan Ernst Matzeliger

Jan Ernst Matzeliger was a Surinamese American inventor. He brought innovation and transformation to the shoe manufacturing industry with his creation of the Lasting Machine. This gadget had the capability of formulating and attaching the body of a shoe to the sole without manual labor. Although his demise came before celebrating the spoils of his labor, the Lasting Machine has been identified in history as a crucial device that significantly impacted American commercialism and society.

Figure 76 10-Year-Old Jan Ernst Matzeliger Working in his Father's Mechanical Shop

Jan Ernst Matzeliger was born on September 15, 1852, in Paramaribo, Dutch Guiana (now known as Suriname), to a wealthy Jewish Dutch father, Ernst Matzeliger, who worked as an engineer, and an unknown Black slave mother. Ernst Matzeliger was a Jewish Dutch who owned colonial ship work and businesses for three generations. Jan's mother was an African slave who worked on the coffee plantation owned by Ernst Matzeliger. At the age of ten, he showed remarkable mechanical aptitude and began to accompany his father and assist him in his mechanical shop.

At the age of nineteen, Jan's father decided it best for him to leave the country, and therefore, he arranged for him to get on a ship to America. Jan was labeled a mulatto, the first-generation offspring of a Black person and a White person. Just like Jan, there were many mulattos in Suriname in those days because of White planters who were sleeping with Black slave women. However, these White planters did not want their biracial children to grow up in a slave environment; therefore, they decided to arrange for their sons to go to America. One of the critical reasons for this was because they knew the situation would backfire once the children discovered they were a product of rape. A great example of these childhood effects was seen in Boni, as he single-handedly destroyed the slave business in Suriname by raging war against the plantations.

The White planters also told their sons to pretend that they were Russians upon arrival in America since they were of lighter complexions. Based on what we have learned from the historical text, their plan backfired. In 1871, Jan set out on his voyage to discover a new world, and after two years of navigation, he settled in Philadelphia to pursue work in the shoe industry after word spread of its growing demand. Having the compound challenge of being foreign and mulatto made it difficult to secure work. Matzeliger's native language was Dutch, and therefore, he struggled with the English language. He decided to attend evening classes to enhance his language skills and learn other scholarly subjects. In 1877, he finally had a breakthrough when he mastered the English language and secured a position as a shoe factory apprentice in Lynn, Massachusetts.

Figure 77 Jan Ernst Matzeliger

In addition to his shoe work, Matzeliger enjoyed painting as a hobby. He was also a religious person, so he attempted to become part of the local Unitarian, Episcopal, and Catholic churches in Lynn, Massachusetts, sadly, to no avail. Consequently, because of the rampant racism within these religious sectors, they shunned the thought of accepting a Negro into their congregation. In 1884, Matzeliger was finally welcomed into the Christian Endeavor Society, the youth wing of the North Congregational Church. At the factory, Jan functioned in a double capacity as both managing shoemaker operator and Sunday school teacher at The North Congregational Church.[186]

Within the Harney Brothers' Shoe Factory, Jan's apprenticeship allowed him to learn the cordwainer trade, a process by which shoes were intricately crafted by hand. The shoes were sized and sculpted with the molds in place. At the end of

---

[186] Henry Louis Gates and Evelyn Brooks Higginbotham, *African American Lives* (New York: Oxford University Press, 2004).

the process, the shoe's body was fixated to the sole manually with "hand lasters." This step was the most challenging and lengthy shoe assembly, as extreme focus and specificity were needed in this final production step. This posed frustration and difficulty within the shoe industry. The production process began with a quick mechanized system, ending with a long, time-consuming manual assembly, creating a holdup and excess in sole production, leaving hand lasters overwhelmed.

While working with a McKay sole-sewing machine, Jan became more enlightened on this problem within the shoe industry. There were no machines capable of, at least that was the perception of industry workers at that time, attaching the top of the shoe to the sole. After carefully studying and observing the hand lasters, Jan began to comprehend the dynamics of affixing the top part of the shoe to the sole and began to create his own strategy for completing the task more efficiently by compiling sketches of machines that may work similarly.

In little to no time, Jan began to produce prototypes of his invention. Despite having insufficient raw materials for use, he mustered together any scraps he could get his hands on, including old pieces of wood, nails, cigar boxes, paper, and scrap wire. After half a year of trial and error, Jan believed he was on the right track, but he needed the appropriate resources to progress forward. As Jan continued to provide enhancements to his invention, his work became fodder for conversation, and he began to receive financial bids up to $1,500. However, the thought of selling his device was unbearable, so Jan negotiated by agreeing to sell a two-thirds interest in his machinery to interested stakeholders, Charles H. Delnow and Melville S. Nichols while keeping the remainder for himself. With his newfound financial surplus, Jan was finally able to complete his work.

Figure 78 Lasting Machine

On March 20, 1883, Jan patented his lasting machine which enabled him to conform a shoe, hammer in the nails, and generate a finished product in a sixty-second timeframe.[187] During ongoing quality improvements, the first public process manifested on May 29, 1885, when his machine defied the odds and surpassed anything else seen to date by lasting 75 pairs of shoes. Feeling confident and reeling from success, Jan, and his original investors, Delnow and Nichols, were able to secure additional funds from Sydney W. Winslow and George A. Brown for increased capital support in producing the lasting machine. As a result of this new advanced partnership, the Consolidated Lasting Machine Company was birthed. Subsequently, Jan sold his patent rights to the investors in turn for catapulting stock. By the end of the 1890s, the Consolidated Lasting Machine Company combined with numerous sub-sized businesses to develop the United Shoe Machinery Corporation, resulting in a monopoly over the U.S. shoe-making industry. Consequently, the company moved on to become a billion-dollar entity.

---

[187] Beverly Bucknor, "Innovative Americans," accessed March 29, 2022, http://www.teacherbulletin.org/media/resources/V01_FullVersion.pdf.

In the summer of 1887, Jan became ill with what first appeared to be a typical cold but later proved to be tuberculosis. Being a determined man, Jan pressed on in the face of failing health, stimulating his mind with attempts at new creations and art as a pastime. Sadly, on August 24, 1889,[188] Jan finally succumbed to his ailment while residing in Lynn, Massachusetts, just one month away from his 37th birthday. However, just before his demise, Matzeliger gave The North Congregational church the majority of his stocks and the rights to his invention. He also made sure that the other denominations that rejected his membership were never partakers of his estate and wealth.

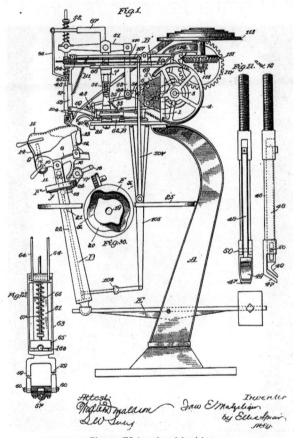

Figure 79 Lasting Machine

---

[188] Sidney Kaplan, "Jan Earnst Matzeliger and the Making of the Shoe," *The Journal of Negro History* 40, no. 1 (1955): pp. 8-33, https://doi.org/10.2307/2715446.

As his life was cut too short, Jan did not have the opportunity to enjoy the spoils of his labor and truly experience the transformation that his lasting machine brought to the shoe industry, producing an unprecedented 700 pairs of shoes daily. Situations were dramatically shifted in a positive direction within the shoe industry, including increased wages and Lynn, Massachusetts being put on the map and marked in history as the shoe capital of the world. Due to the magnitude of Matzeliger's invention, many did not want to accept or acknowledge that Matzeliger was a Black man. A certified copy of his death certificate had to be presented to confirm what had already been known by the masses; the invention of a Black man from Suriname transformed the shoe industry.[189]

Figure 80 Jan E. Matzeliger U.S.A Postage Stamp

---

[189] David Eugene Wharton, *The Engineering and Technological Education of Black Americans: 1865-1950* (Amherst, MA: University of Massachusetts Amherst, 2019).

Postmortem, Jan Ernst Matzeliger was acknowledged for his significant works and was given the Gold Medal and Diploma at the Pan-American Exposition of 1901. Over a half-century later, in 1967, a radio drama sequence entitled "The Great Ones" executed a broadcast headlining Jan's life journey. Thereafter, the US. Postal Service commemorated Jan Ernst Matzeliger by issuing a unique stamp memorializing him in 1991 as a piece of the Black Heritage collection.

Daddy by the Pikin Mma Kiiki (Small Mother Creek)

This is the story of my dad on Pikin Mma Kiiki. My dad had an interesting childhood. Dad was only 10 years old when he started working with his stepdad. My paternal grandparents divorced when my dad was a toddler. This resulted in my grandfather departing his wife's village and returning to his native village. This was usually the tradition among Ndyuka men, possessing homes in multiple villages. My grandmother remarried, and dad referred to his stepdad as *mi D'a* (my dad). His stepdad was a lumberjack, and since my dad was not allowed to attend school, he had to go and help his stepdad cut lumber. They would transport the lumber long distance through the dense woods of the Cottica forest to the nearest creek to get to the Cottica River. Dad woke up each morning at 4:00 AM so he and his stepdad could hit the road with their lantern to travel by canoe, and then, on foot. In the 1930s, there was no electricity, no cars, or roads, the only form of transportation was to travel on foot or by canoe.

Dad cultivated a strong work ethic while working with his stepdad. I remember dad telling us how he would wake up early in the morning, rain, or shine, and make this journey into the jungle. There were instances when he would work in wet clothes all day, towing wood, sometimes through mud, swampland, and dense jungle, just to get the wood to the river. This daily routine would continue for years until dad's late teenage years.

One afternoon, as Dad and his stepdad were crossing one of the creeks to get to the village, something remarkable happened. His stepdad stopped the canoe and began to tell him the story of the creek that they were on. His stepdad paused for a second as he stopped the boat and said, "*Bia*," meaning "young man", as it was a custom to refer to young men as *bia* in the Ndyuka culture. My dad answered, "*Abii Mi D'a*," meaning "yes my daddy." His stepdad said, "Do you know the history of this creek that we are on right now?" and dad answered, "No, I do not. All I know is that this is part of the Cottica River." His stepdad replied to him and said, "No, this is not part of the Cottica River. This is a separate creek. Before my dad passed away, he informed me that during the slavery era, he was one of the slaves that dug the creek." My dad replied and said, "You mean someone dug this entire river?", and he said, "Yes." With tears of pain trickling down his cheek, he said, "The creek that we are on right now is called *Pikin Mma*, dug by slaves, and my father helped dig it. They had to do this every day, from sunrise to sunset. My dad started weeping as well, because he could not imagine the creek being dug by hand, based on the width, length, and depth of the creek. At that moment, they both took time to weep, because they felt an inner pain of what their ancestors, and in this case, his own father, had to go through during the time of slavery. That moment sparked an epiphany in their lives. From that day forward, it became a tradition that each day, as they would pass through that creek, they would stop and sometimes just tear up, because they considered that place sacred ground. Out of reverence, they would pause before they moved along their daily journey. Years later, Dad took ill in the village and experienced a long road to recovery. In his early 20s, Dad finally left the village and moved to the capital of Paramaribo for a better life. He was among one of the first Ndyuka who left the village to live in the big city. He later worked for the American bauxite company, took early retirement, and established his own bus company.

Petrus Domini The Game Changer:
The Man who Helped Permanently Shape and Transform the Political Climate in Suriname.

Uncle Petrus was one of my favorite uncles, and he used to visit my dad often at his Paramaribo residence. Uncle Petrus used to have long talks with my dad. He was very talkative, and there was never a dull moment when he was visiting. From childhood, every time Uncle Petrus would stop by for a visit, my brother and I would ask him to have a sleepover at his house. One evening, as Uncle Petrus was preparing to head home, my brother and I pleaded, once again, to go to his house for a sleepover, and this time he decided to take us. Halfway there, we started crying and told him we wanted to go home. I remember Uncle Petrus had driven a reasonable distance, but we were crying because we wanted to go back home. Without hesitation, void of anger or wrath, Uncle Petrus told us to be patient; he would turn around and take us back to mom and dad. Uncle Petrus was a thoughtful man with a caring heart.

Uncle Petrus was also a man of vision, having foresight into the future, unlike many of his peers. He had a strong vision for the Ndyuka people. He wanted to see them advance and thrive, not only in the interior, within their domain, but to influence both a national and international level. In 1973, two years before Suriname's independence from the Netherlands, Uncle Petrus came up with an idea to create a political party for the Ndyuka people, mainly those who were residing on the Cottica River. He was very excited and passionate about bringing that vision to fruition. Uncle Petrus knew that it would be crucial to have a voice as Ndyuka people after gaining independence, so he thought ahead to make provisions for that voice to manifest. He also knew that success would only occur through a well-established political party coming from the interior. With that unity, Uncle Petrus could ignite a voice in the decision-making of the advancement of the Ndyuka people and the country or nation at large.

Figure 81 Petrus Domini, Founder of The Suriname Political Party, The General Liberation and Development Party (Algemene Bevrijdings en Ontwikkelingspartij) ABOP

He took his vision to one of the core places in Cottica, which is my mother's village called Pina-tjarimi (Pina Tjai Mi Kon Ya), (meaning *famine brought me here*) on the Cottica River. Pina-tjarimi village is also referred to as Da-Dyemesi Kondee (Da-Dyemesi Village) because it was founded by her great-great-uncle called Da-Dyemesi, because he said, "I was starving, and because I was starving where I was, I moved to this place so that I would not have to starve anymore." Symbolically, Uncle Petrus knew it was time for the Ndyuka people to thrive as well, instead of looking for handouts from those who were in power, namely the government. That is why he chose that sacred dwelling place. Uncle Petrus proceeded to meet with a group of Cotticaners to discuss his vision of establishing a political party. To his amazement, he ran into strong opposition from his fellow Cotticaners, who did not believe in his concepts and, therefore, did not support his theories and endeavors. Uncle Petrus was further advised by Mr. John Molien, a fellow Cotticaner, to extinguish his plan of establishing a party. As a result, Uncle Petrus did not receive the expected support from his fellow Ndyuka people to establish the political party. He did not, however, see this refusal as defeat. Although he was

194

disappointed in his fellow Ndyuka people, Uncle Petrus took this as an encouragement to keep on fighting for the advancement of the Ndyuka people, and that experience and perseverance helped him progress in his political career. Meanwhile, the anguish in this ordeal was that 1) Uncle Petrus' Ndyuka community did not understand the power of politics and, 2) the Ndyuka failed to see the influence that they as Ndyuka people could have at the decision-making table. Instead, they misconstrued Uncle Petrus' vision and ideas and labeled him as a con man. That label became a stigma within his family for the next several decades. Since his last name was Domini, it negatively affected others that held the same last name. Fellow Ndyukas considered those with the last name Domini as con artists. There was also a popular saying that the Dominis were not trustworthy but rather political. Growing up, I heard the statement, "The Dominis are political" regularly. I remember, as a young man, I was invited to speak somewhere, and in the middle of my speech I mentioned my name, someone stood up in the crowd and said, "Oh, you are a Domini! We do not know if we can work with you because your people are very political!" I did not know the exact words to use to defend myself, but as I became more mature, I realized that for all my life, spanning over four decades, that statement used against the Dominis was completely wrong and out of context. What the people who spread this falsehood did not realize was that my uncle, Petrus Domini, was not a con artist. He was not a deceiver because he had the vision to enter politics, but he was a visionary, and he saw things that his colleagues deemed impossible. It took the Ndyuka people, as a community, more than four decades after Uncle Petrus shared his vision for them to grasp his notion of having a solid political party. They finally deciphered that this was not for selfish gain but to benefit the totality of the Maroon people in Suriname. This delayed revelation was not an insult to the Dominis but merely a lack of knowledge. Consequently, can you imagine if the Maroon people, two years before the independence of Suriname, had formulated a political party that possessed the power to participate in the decision-making of the development of the nearly independent state of Suriname? Ndyuka people would have been far more advanced and would have had a stronger voice in the execution of policy and socioeconomic processes. Instead, we slacked and missed decades of advancement and life-transforming opportunities due to our deficient foresight, fear of change, or fear of what may have been perceived as radical thinking.

In 1973, Uncle Petrus was not alone in his political battle. It was also the year that the BEP, *Broederschap en Eenheid in de Politiek* (Brotherhood and Unity in Politics), was established. The political party, BEP, had an ideology and mindset that focused on the people of the interior of Suriname. As a young political party, they attempted to enter their first election with the established Progressive National Party (PNP), but the negotiation between both parties failed. Subsequently, in November 1973, the newly founded BEP entered the election for the first time as an independent party. They had a well-structured team of candidates in Paramaribo, the capital, in addition to Brokopondo and Marowijne, where Petrus Domini served as a candidate. Although it was well-structured, the party neglected to secure any seat in government. Once more, we see that the leaders failed because they did not receive the endorsement of the Maroon community. Thereafter, the BEP continued to participate in all elections and managed to gain a few seats in government, yet still did not gain ultimate power status. This was partially due to the insufficient outreach to the Maroon people at large. It was evident that the outreach was ineffective since the majority of outreach took place close to an election cycle, instead of it being an ongoing initiative. Thus, the Maroon people were not collectively reached and groomed to be followers of the party's philosophies nor educated about the benefits that came with a collective win. In essence, the party was dormant but would spring seasonally, which constituted a lack of growth. Where there is a lack of growth, there is also a lack of accomplishment. This created a major barrier to mass outreach. Uncle Petrus saw the void and inactivity of the party and therefore decided to part ways.

The Establishment of ABOP Algemene Bevrijdings en Ontwikkelingspartij (The General Liberation and Development Party)

Uncle Petrus often talked about politics and government. When Uncle Petrus visited dad, there were instances when strangers would accompany him, and they would talk about various types of politics. Sometimes people from other countries would be present, speaking English, and at that time, I had no clue what they were talking about. I did, nevertheless, find it interesting because Uncle Petrus was a fast talker and very passionate in delivery. He had a natural ability to persuade you to adopt his beliefs. In the late 1980s, Uncle Petrus approached dad and shared the idea of reactivating the defunct BEP political party. He also told dad that he did not have a place to host his meetings. Dad immediately filled the void by allowing Uncle Petrus to hold his meetings right in his living room on Jowjow Straat (Jowjow Street). They started to have regular meetings at my dad's house from that day on until my uncle and his party members found an official meeting place.

In that same year, Uncle Petrus proceeded to find the general liberation and development party, ABOP. Many individuals from the BEP and the PBP, a now-retired political party, made various attempts to thwart Uncle Petrus from the development of the new party, explicitly to restore and preserve the unity within the BEP party. Uncle Petrus was gung-ho in maintaining his decision to launch the ABOP party. ABOP became a solidified party and started gaining influence among the Maroon people at large. The BEP party made several attempts to unite both parties and failed four consecutive times, as they could not agree on certain policies, interests, and visions not directly aligned with that of Uncle Petrus.

The Transition

In 1987, Uncle Petrus founded the general liberation and development party, ABOP, and continued with members of his party and the Ndyuka people to impact the elections. They also made significant progress within the party and the party outreach. Uncle Petrus was officially established as the party chairman in 1990. After six years, a transition would take place after Ronnie Brunswijk; the ex-jungle commando leader would join the party. Brunswijk was very interested in the leadership of the party, as he was transitioning into politics. He had a great interest in politics because he gaged that politics would afford him better outreach to the Maroon people, and with that interest, he approached Uncle Petrus to inquire about party leadership. Ronnie Brunswijk was not a stranger to Uncle Petrus, as they were family members. Additionally, Uncle Petrus knew that with Ronnie Brunswijk on the team, they could accomplish a great deal within the politics of Suriname. Hence, Ronnie Brunswijk became the second party treasurer in 1996. After a lengthy discussion between Ronnie Brunswijk and Uncle Petrus, Uncle Petrus had to make a major decision about whether he should continue as chairman of the party or allow Brunswijk to become chair of the party. Uncle Petrus knew that the party would continue a path of stability and progression if he maintained chairmanship. On the other hand, handing the party over would be the fortitude of Brunswijk to catapult the party to the next level. Uncle Petrus gave himself ample time to weigh his decision as to whether he should relinquish the party or not. After much consideration and mediation, Uncle Petrus decided to secede the party's leadership to Ronnie Brunswijk.

Ronnie Brunswijk then became the new party chairman and began to work rapidly. Brunswijk did not hesitate but precipitated to participate in his first election since becoming chairman. Although he did not earn any seat in the cabinet, that did not stop him from pursuing more options of becoming part of parliament.

In Brunswijk's second election, in conjunction with other political parties, he successfully attained five seats. Brunswijk continued to make progress with the party, and he would then get his major break in the 2020 election, where he teamed with other political parties to form one ticket, securing a collective win. This win placed ABOP in an advantageous position.

For the first time in Suriname's political history, the Maroons managed to achieve the pinnacle of politics. Even though previous years of Maroon people possessed high positions in Surinamese politics and the cabinet, 2020 was the very first time that Maroon people, namely Ndyuka people, acquired a vice-presidential position, the national assembly chair position, and many ministerial positions in the cabinet. This was a breakthrough for every Maroon person, in and outside of Suriname, to be able to lead the effort of the highest office of the land. However, the Maroon people were criticized by other ethnic groups for this great achievement, as though they were either not capable of or not educated enough to perform in such a great governmental capacity.

Make no mistake, the Maroon people are proud of such an honor, reminding them that although they were brought to Suriname as slaves, they did not remain conceded to slavery. They emancipated themselves, and they continue to live, thrive, and maintain their culture in the jungle. After 400 years, the Maroon people in Suriname gained the power to become key decision-makers in the politics of Suriname. In the end, Uncle Petrus was correct in his decision to relinquish the party to Brunswijk, who indeed took the party not just to another level but was able to develop expanded outreach to the Maroon society and beyond. As for the Maroon people, with this great accomplishment, there are endless opportunities to be part of the ruling entities within the Surinamese political system and abroad. It is up to the different Maroon political parties in Suriname to maintain the progress and unity in their parties and represent well within the politics of Suriname.

As a Ndyuka myself, I think the most effective way for the Maroon people to continue to excel in politics is to continue to enhance one voice as a people and strengthen their unity. Although that is the efficient way to operate in order to enjoy an ongoing victory, it's not easy to realize this idea, but it's possible. One of the main steps that need to be taken is that parties must be able and willing to compromise by putting some party interests and ideologies aside and adopting that which will enhance the totality versus one individual party or concept. With that idea esteemed as the highest ideal, the Maroon parties will thrive and profit from an ongoing victory and governance at the higher level.

CHAPTER 11

TRUE REVOLUTION OF FREE

MALOGASSI

"Mi fii fu katibo"

(I am free from bondage)

F reedom is not free. The revolution of true freedom is the experience and the absence of subjection to domination and an imprisonment state of being. The cry for freedom is a cry that every human being has at their core. Freedom is part of the human DNA and existence. There is something that constantly attests and confirms that we were born to be free. The moment freedom is absent, meaning that there is a violation in the human experience and existence, one will resist the oppression and fight to gain that missing component that caused him or her to lose their independence.

Humans will inevitably fight at any cost and with every fiber of their being to be free, even to the point of death. The Ndyuka people in Suriname knew their freedom was both jeopardized and violated at every possible level, and their existence was willfully dismissed in the most gruesome ways. The anguish was to the point that one would give up on life and declare that life was not worth living. Sometimes the question may be why one individual would eliminate the rights and privileges of another for their benefit and ambition, with absolutely no regard to their existence. The answer is many people seek self-ambition and self-gratification, wanting to see themselves progress and advance in life, regardless of how the other person feels. Once they can advance, that is all that matters. The reality is that there is something deep inside each one of us that will always fight for our right to be free. Being free means:

- Having the ability to make decisions for oneself.
- Having the power and ability to empower oneself and others.
- Having the flexibility of mobility without any restraint.
- Having the privilege to embark on new horizons.
- The exploration of new opportunities.
- Having the self-determination to accomplish goals set.

- Resilience: the power and ability to recover quickly from difficulties.
- Feeling an experience of liberation.
- Being emancipated and enjoying the fruits thereof.
- Having the ability to determine your journey and destination.
- The power of self-governance.

If we talk about slavery, we must discuss it from a mental, physical, and spiritual perspective. Physical captivity can seize your body, but it does not have to capture your mind and spirit. Although it may affect your mind and spirit negatively, it does not have to determine the actions taken in your mind and in your spirit. The Ndyukas were captured and restrained, but one thing was not captured, and that was their mind and their spirit. They were determined to have their mind and spirit intact. They used their minds to strategize well-thought-out plans on how to make their experience on the plantations bearable and how to escape the horrific situation of their current existence. As they were going through this execution plan over and over in their minds, with a spirit of determination, regardless of the confinement and restriction of their bodies, they were finally able to put their plan into action.

The mindset of self-determination was present. With self-determination to go beyond the restriction and the hurdles that lay in front of them, the Ndyukas were able to reach out, grab the opportunity, and exercise their innate rights and power that could not be diminished to set themselves free. They were shackled from head to toe by their hands, feet, and neck, but they were liberated in their minds because the shackles did not blind the view of independence. They were independent in their minds long before they experienced the independence of their bodies. In other words, the strength that the Ndyukas had in becoming free and independent people was unstoppable. The battle was already won, and freedom was already attained in their minds. The sense of liberation and emancipation was already established. Therefore, the execution was just a matter of time. Nothing else on the plantation, nor the road to freedom, would stop the Ndyukas or serve as a stumbling block for them to be free.

The Ndyukas were still on the plantation, yet they could see a new world and a new life of freedom. Their mindset was already emancipated. They were slaves physically but were unconfined mentally. They walked every day as slaves, but inside, they preserved their dignity and mental state of being as free men. Others saw the Ndyukas as enslaved people, but they saw themselves as unrestrained and independent. Others saw the Ndyukas as imprisoned people, but they perceived themselves as kings and queens, people of great worth and dignity. Others saw the Ndyukas as unlettered and uneducated people, but they saw themselves as great inventors with extraordinary intellect. Mental slavery never regulated them because they were already liberated in their minds before they self-emancipated their bodies.

The spiritual aspect of the Ndyukas' lives was that they communicated with the supernatural being referred to as Gaan Gadu (God). They often referred to their ancestors with the strong belief of going before them and clearing the path or making way for them to have a successful life. One thing slavery and oppression could not do to them is take away their faith and belief in the highest God. They knew how to pray...they had strong faith. They knew how to cry because they knew that God was the only one who could hear them where no one could hear them, so therefore they never lost sight of having God on their side. Spirituality was key in the life of these captured Africans. You can kill the body, but you cannot kill the spirit.

They kept their spirits uplifted by creating songs, inspirational songs, songs that would lift them up in those hours of oppression. There was no freedom of speech. They could not talk back to the plantation owners. They could not reason because they were seen as inferior. They were considered half-human, half-animal, and therefore, they were treated like animals. However, they knew that they had freedom of speech to talk to God. They could voice their opinion, their cries, and their petition to God. They had no liberty to talk to each other sometimes because of distrust, and oftentimes there was no loyalty amongst each other, in and outside of the plantation, but they could trust God to share their emotions and their concerns, knowing that He would not betray them. He would not go back and tell the wrong person about their shortcomings or their plans and intentions. Furthermore, He would not only keep it to Himself, but He would indeed bring a solution to that matter.

Spirituality as a major part of the Africans had to come to fruition for them to survive. They knew that they were doomed or set up for destruction because the paths of their lives were already determined for them by the slave traders, and there was no other way around it. There was no other expectation for them to live a decent human life. Therefore, they knew that their freedom would depend on different factors, making their spirituality crucial. Their spirit would not allow them to settle for less nor yield to the request of what was expected from them. The more they were brutalized, the more their spirits were quickened and alerted them to fight. There was some spiritual component that would cause them to fight the oppression, fight the pain, and fight the atrocity, so their spirit was fueled by the pain that they had to go through to fight oppression. There was nowhere in the world where these captured Africans would stop fighting because what the oppressors did not know was that their oppression of their oppressed was the fuel to their spirit to fight their oppressors. The ignorance of the oppressor was the strength of the oppressed.

Negro spiritual songs were born as an extended part of their African songs that they turned into words of encouragement, affirmation, empowerment, hidden messages, and secret codes. These Negro spirituals were prophetic songs that spoke to the core of them, knowing that they needed God's strength to survive. They needed the strength of God to endure, endure the pain and the brutality. Without a shadow of a doubt, they knew that they needed a higher power to ease their pain and give them the strength to take the next step tomorrow. Whether it was songs that referred to God or songs that referred to their ancestors, they knew that they had to lean on those that have gone before them. They continuously uplifted and upheld traditions of old that were imparted to them. Those traditions were the knowledge and strength and hidden secrets that they brought with them from Africa. They knew how to preserve the knowledge that they acquired from the motherland.

During the era of slavery, Africans have fought and have constantly pushed back the feeling of oppression, the feeling of being eliminated. Their emotions were quenched, and the rights to express their emotions were violated. They found themselves in an environment of controlled emotion. How to love, how and when to speak, and how to express their feelings were all under complete control, so much so that it had psychological effects. When your oppressor controls emotion, it makes way for psychological infringement. They knew that they were placed in an atmosphere that was conducive to keeping them in emotional bondage. Therefore, they fought and pushed so hard to be emotionally free. They did so if it meant refusing orders, deliberately disobeying their plantation owners, or taking off into the jungle and risking their lives; they were not in it to lose their minds. Emotional freedom has been fought throughout the era of slavery in many places and countries, including the United States, where people of color have not only fought for physical freedom but emotional freedom too.

The Emotional Impact of Slavery on the African American People

The path towards acceptance, healing, and emotional stability among African Americans over the years has not been a simple one. Up to today, the issue of slavery has been a source of emotional weakness and grief among the Black community. The legacy of slavery coupled with discrimination has a continued impact on African Americans' social and economic stability. Many African Americans still cling to the thoughts that transfix them to the impacts of slavery and discrimination at the expense of White supremacy in the country. The impacts of racism and slavery have led to constant feelings of anger, low regard for self, and outrage among African American communities in various parts of the United States.

Figure 82 Protesting Racism in The United States

The image of the Whites created a platform for unjust actions that have lasted for centuries in the Americas since the 15th century. Millions of African Americans have suffered the experience of being subjected to mistreatment at the hands of their fellow men. Some theoretical views depict slavery as a major force that has caused African Americans to draw a clear picture of inhumanity among other races, especially Whites in the United States. At the same time, the impacts of racism and slavery caused socio-economic instability and imbalances with other races in the United States. Even today, many African American communities in the United States lag behind their White counterparts due to being confined by the pressures of poverty, low income, unemployment, poor living standards, and other socio-economic disadvantages. Most of these issues are associated with the histories of these communities that involve slavery, racism, discrimination, and prejudice.

Despite all these forces and challenges for African Americans, the church has acted as an agent of social reform and a source of survival among these communities. At the same time, the church has acted as an institution that has helped African Americans to shape their views of the White people in the country. Through the church, African Americans have embraced resilience and forged social ties in their localities and across the nation. This has enabled them to overcome adversity. Also, resilience has helped communities and individuals to maintain positive mental health that is free from thoughts about past experiences in slavery, racism, discrimination, and prejudice. The Black church has and still serves as an instrument and buffer that has provided mental strength and life meaning among African Americans. At the same time, it has helped bridge the social gaps that previously existed among African Americans and other races in the United States. Therefore, slavery has contributed to the rise of church and religious activities among African American communities. This has helped erase the memories and feelings of hatred, anger, and outrage due to past painful experiences. Human pain will always create an outcome for a true solution.

The writing of the Ndyuka Land book was a literary journey for me. This journey led me to organize meetings with community leaders and church leaders, plan events and seminars, and allowed me to engage and connect with diverse people from all walks of life. Through this experience, I was able to learn and gain valuable resources on leadership and community empowerment. The impact of slavery on the community and how we can learn and help improve our community in response to this knowledge is a message resonating within the Black community. What I found most impactful in creating the pages of this book is the art of storytelling, where storytellers and elders alike came together to tell their personal stories as part of the healing process, creating an atmosphere of transparency, growth, and upliftment.

Ndyuka Land was published to impact the world. This book is a project that will not only affect or impact this generation but will impact future generations to come. To speak of Africans who self-emancipated themselves, fled into the jungle, and lived there while maintaining their African traditions and culture as a free people is a refreshing twist in society. Most of the traditional slavery stories we know have all been about the harsh punishment and suffering endured by slaves. This story provides a different depiction of Africans living as normal people outside of Africa, enjoying their freedom. It is intended for every human to live in physical, spiritual, and mental freedom.

Beyond the Shadow

My goal in writing this book is for people to feel liberated, enlightened, hopeful, free, and genuinely happy when reading the pages of this historic voyage. This book is not a book to mourn slavery, but it is a book to bring awareness that while other nations and people were enslaved, there were a group of Africans that stood up and fought for their rights. A group of Africans escaped the horror and atrocity that could happen to their fellow Africans. Brothers and sisters, this book sheds light on wholeness, freedom, liberty, and justice for all. The call to action for this book is not to focus on where we have been, and it is not even to focus on where we have come from, but to concentrate on where we are and where we are heading. The future of hope rests upon the fact that we cannot look back and have self-pity, rage, or anger because of our ancestral past. Yes, slavery is part of our history, and we must acknowledge it, but our response should not be actions of anger and rage. Rather, let us employ an act of celebration, an act of giving, hope to the hopeless, and an act of helping to unshackle others from mental bondage.

The time and era of pointing our finger at those who oppressed us in the past are long gone. As a people, we should not wait for people to bring us to the table but instead create our own, and in turn, build seats at the table to bring others alongside us. The importance of uniting as a village, with collaboration and different strengths coming together as one, is the true catalyst to creating sustainable change in our communities. We mustn't live in isolation, nor fight with one another, but join collectively, whether you are Black, White, or indigenous, regardless of color or origin, because as one, we can accomplish more than operating as single entities.

We cannot continuously dwell on former turmoil, but we must rise and progress as a nation. We must sound the alarm of freedom and fight for sovereignty and justice just like our fellow runaway and self-emancipated Africans in Suriname continuously fought for their freedom, which they indeed maintained along with their African culture. Those of African descent in the diaspora, embrace and adopt the culture of the country you are living in, but never lose sight of your roots. You are an African, and Africa is still in you.

It is important to be reminded that your external circumstances do not dictate your success and destination in life. By understanding your internal identity, nothing can deter you from becoming successful in life. Not even the environment you are in now can determine your success, but understanding your identity, and who you truly are will cause you to thrive in life. Just like the runaway and self-emancipated Africans, the Ndyuka people in Suriname did not allow their circumstances and their environments of captivity to keep them in prison or enslaved, but they knew who they were; they were warriors and kings and free people that were imprisoned against their will, so they were determined to liberate and emancipate themselves by any means necessary. They took this journey to unchartered territory, risking whatever it takes, risking their lives, and through multiple attempts, they succeeded. It's our civil, moral, and social obligation to keep on fighting for what is right, what is just, what is commendable, what is relevant, what is honorable, what is dignified, what is courageous, and what is peaceful for all human beings no matter what your creed is. Justice for all and freedom for all.

The Fear That Prevents Freedom

The path to freedom is a tedious one, yet takes an enormous amount of courage and determination. It is not for the weak at heart. Fear is always present when you are on the brink of freedom. Fear is a component that is necessary to activate your faith, courage, willpower, determination, and action. It is the type of fear that changes your mental state of mind. The type of fear that is so enormous that it reaches its max; in other words, it cannot go beyond where it is...that is where you know that you are in transition. You are in the time of action. You fear until you cannot fear anymore. Your fear is full (fearful) and there is nothing beyond this point to fear. It was former President of the United States, Franklin D. Roosevelt, that said, "The only thing we have to fear is fear itself."

I believe my Ndyuka ancestors said, "You fear until there is nothing else to fear" over and over in their minds and verbally. As Boni, the freedom fighter, and those that were with him would proclaim, "I would rather die and be dilapidated into dust than to be on the plantation." Boni and his group were ready to pay the ultimate price for freedom. Fear did not stop them from going back and raiding the plantations and taking with them men, women, and children regularly. Unfortunately, some were so captured by fear that they refused to leave the plantation. For them, it was easier to be there and go through the inhumane treatment than to escape to freedom. This is the irony of fear. Although you know that there is a better outcome and better life circumstances, the paralytic effect of fear is so strong that it not only holds you captive, but it causes you to miss out on a life full of freedom, a life full of greatness, a life full of expectations, a life full of resources and opportunities, and freedom itself. What we can learn today is the valuable lesson that although our life circumstances may not be remotely close to that of those on the plantation, we must turn our fear into action, meaning that we have to take the necessary steps not to allow our fear to eliminate our path to freedom. All human beings have the right to enjoy their freedom. Therefore, you must know that it is your moral responsibility to fight for your freedom. Do not allow the fear of repercussion to stop you. It is easy to stay in a detrimental situation, whether it is an abusive relationship, work, relationship, or a contract, but the truth is, the only reason why you are still there is for fear of repercussion. You can be so captured by fear that you would rather endure that horrific circumstance than face the outcome of retaliation. For some, the comfort of the norm, even if it is dysfunction, is better than the unknown. Step out, take action, breathe, conquer, and fly. These are words that you must take into consideration and act upon to experience your freedom. You can live in absolute freedom. Consider the price and go for it.

CHAPTER 12

A CALL TO ACTION

"Meke wi leli fafu libi anga wi seefi"

(Let us learn how to live with one another)

The Ndyuka people from Suriname have been known for their resiliency and extra surviving skills. They are inevitably equipped with such extraordinary skills because from the moment they were captured and sold in Africa and taken past the point of no return, they knew they had entered unchartered waters. The horrifying slave ship experience across the Atlantic Ocean helped mold and shape the kidnapped Africans' way of thinking. Furthermore, the new world, where they were resold to the new plantation owners, heightened the Africans' awareness. Not only had they set sail from their homeland, but they were also separated from home, not knowing when and if they would ever return. The Ndyuka people managed to lean on the survival skills they learned back in Africa through this ordeal. Up to this point, all they knew was to learn more ways to survive as they fled into the deep, dense jungle away from the plantation, where they established a new life for themselves.

Living in A Mixed Society

After such a traumatic experience of four hundred years of continuous pressure and torture as a group of people, the Ndyuka people had to deal with the colonial planters and their soldiers, during their time on the plantation and their time on the run and after the abolition of slavery. They had to learn to cohabitate and coexist with former colonial planters, ex-slaves, non-slaves, and the immigrants that came to Suriname as migrant workers. This was a new experience of reconciliation and trust they had to build with people they once considered their enemy, but this was not such an easy transition for both the Ndyukas and non-Ndyuka people. Even though the Ndyuka people lived as free people in the jungle for over a century before the abolition of slavery, after slavery ended, they had to endure racial, economic, and educational disparities. The

Ndyuka people had to breach the racial gap of prejudices from the non-Ndyukas, as they often were considered the lowest among all races in Suriname. The Ndyuka and other Maroon tribes of Suriname have had a long history of intersectionality, which refers to the multifaceted discrimination experienced by individuals who belong to multiple minority groups.

Overcoming Racism and Adversity

"I have a dream that one day this nation will rise up and live out the true meaning of its creed. We hold these truths to be self-evident, that all men are created equal." This is part of what Dr. Martin Luther King, Jr.'s said in his *I Have a Dream* speech. He had a vision and eloquently inserted this immortal declaration in his speech. Freedom is in the DNA of all living beings; the absence of freedom is chaos because there is a void. The Ndyuka people have experienced decades of racial discrimination and racial inequity, but they have learned along the way to overcome by taking necessary steps that will ultimately lead to a change. The first step was education because they were in the jungle for so long; there was no access to public education, and that caused them to miss out on participating on a greater scale and national platform. Due to the disparity, the rest of the people of Suriname did not count the Ndyuka people as educated, and consequently, they did not have a seat at the table with the so-called scholars and change-makers. They were not considered part of the decision-making factors in the international operations of Suriname as a country. That narrative has changed in recent years because the Ndyukas have understood the dynamics of education and development. With that elevated mindset, they took education by storm. Within the Ndyuka and Maroon community, they began to produce well-educated and eloquent individuals. Education and public schooling became paramount within the Ndyuka community. The understanding and the opportunity for higher education became more prevalent. There were more college graduates with terminal degrees. With the former traditional knowledge of oral education and formal education combined, the Ndyuka people have established a plethora of knowledge where the rest of the community was forced to give them a place at the table. In every area of society today, Ndyukas are playing a significant role because so many of them are heads of state. Recently, the last election in 2020 showed the diversity and inclusivity of the Surinamese people. The Ndyuka people have reached a height as never before in politics; the Vice-President is a Ndyuka, the head of the National Assembly chairman is a Ndyuka, and Ndyukas hold many other governmental ministerial positions. Many Ndyuka people have developed great entrepreneurial skills and have managed to establish multiple companies. Even in the interior, they owned many businesses. The Ndyuka people have managed to generate multiple streams of income, giving them a great financial advantage. The stigma and stereotyping of Ndyuka people as uneducated, black and ugly, lazy, dangerous, and other demeaning connotations have been disproven. It has been established that Ndyuka people are the most loving, loyal, beautiful, well-educated people you will ever meet. Ndyuka people are well-respected nationally and internationally and are known for their cultural pride. These five words define the Ndyuka: faith, endurance, resilience, intelligence, and intuitiveness.

The Ndyuka and the African American

In my personal view, just like the Ndyuka people from Suriname suffered in the aftermath of slavery, so did the people in the United States; more so, people of color suffered the atrocities of slavery and the rippling effects of the post-slavery era tremendously. People of color in the States today are still fighting for the healing process and healing from the past. The question now is, "Is it possible for people of color in the United States to be healed from their past experiences and current events?" If so, what are the steps to be undertaken? Healing is a process, meaning that a series of actions must be taken towards wholeness. One will have to change their mindset, which means their mentality to be susceptible, to embrace the readily available healing. The healing must come from a deep place of consciousness, a place that requires an inner sincerity and focus that will ultimately translate into outer expression.

It must also be known that healing as a group of people will need to have a different approach versus healing of the nation or country in its entirety. For example, many people of color have considered themselves victimized, disenfranchised, marginalized, and therefore feel the urge to keep themselves separated or alienated. They feel the need to alienate themselves from those they think were or are responsible for such issues. These deep-rooted issues must first be relinquished to adopt true success and healing. If true success and healing were not the blueprints of what you had to follow, then one must do everything in their power to acquire that. That is why it is essential to understand that if you are in a war, you must understand the language and the mindset of your adversary. You must learn to strategize to be able to play on their field. Furthermore, you must learn what makes the other successful and apply those same principles and use them to your advantage. It is not a Black or White mindset that will cause one to experience healing and become successful, but a winning mindset that requires extensive strategizing. In other words, we must strategize and re-strategize, leading to ultimate healing and success. It must be known that healing and true success is a foreign language to the sick and poor. Therefore, one must adapt and learn to speak the language.

Know Yourself: Improving Diversity of The Work and Public Sector

Systemic racism has existed in the U.S. for the longest time. It is often seen as the very foundation of the American state. There are numerous instances where police would be called to investigate a Black man who went jogging, sat in particular cafes, or even lived in a particular neighborhood that was considered a Black neighborhood. Today, America has yet to reconcile with its racist past. There are numerous police brutality cases, particularly Black men and women dying at the hands of law enforcement. This, therefore, begs the question, "Do people of color in the U.S. continue to pay a deadly price from institutions built on White supremacy?" How can we change this narrative as a nation?

From watching the activities around discrimination and racial justice, I have learned that every individual has a role to play in ensuring that people are self-aware of the things surrounding them and that they work towards achieving diversity both in the workplace and social settings. Knowing oneself is an essential skill that every individual needs to learn. It involves understanding personal goals and ambitions, identifying personal biases, and ways through which they can be resolved. This goes a long way in ensuring that social and racial stereotypes are demystified and that racial justice is realized.

Knowing oneself is one of the most important steps that individuals need to take in a bid to end racism in the country. Knowing oneself sometimes involves understating one's roots and childhood experiences, understanding interpersonal and interracial differences, and ensuring that one is open-minded when dealing with people who are different from themselves. Knowing oneself is also very important in ensuring that people make better decisions. There is also less inner conflict and greater self-control when people understand who they are and what it takes to live in a mixed society. Tolerance and understanding for others are also built when people take their time to understand their social differences.

Diversity often results in hostility in the workplace, diversity implementation challenges, and failure to realize goals and objectives in the workplace. There are further barriers to diversity and inclusion in the workplace, including workplace culture, racial stereotypes, and the lack of forward-looking leaders who are willing to deal with existing racial discrimination cases.[190] Understanding all these hurdles is vital in ensuring that long-lasting solutions are identified in the workplace. It is further worth noting that discrimination in the workplace is often undervalued,

---

[190] Gavan Titley and John Wrench, "Managing Diversity, Fighting Racism or Combating Discrimination? A Critical Exploration," in *Resituating Culture* (Strasbourg Cedex: Council of Europe Pub., 2004), pp. 113-133.

and it is reflected in social places and the community at large. Therefore, there is a need to take positive steps towards ensuring that these problems are resolved and that social justice in the workplace is restored.

Racial diversity in the workplace is important because it allows people to have a variety of ideas and perspectives. This ideally results in better interactions and ultimately in the realization of organizational goals and objectives. A diverse workforce often contributes greatly to a diverse community and, most importantly, to a society that understands the importance of social integration. Therefore, it is imperative to ensure that these small steps towards realizing social integration begin in the workplace and are carried on in other social places. This will play a significant role in changing the narrative of racial discrimination that has dominated America for the longest time. Diversity is also crucial in a society because it allows individuals to have different perspectives about certain ideas and, more notably, increases productivity in the workplace. The knowledge that people can slowly change the world by embracing diversity and taking small steps towards making the world a better place by embracing diversity is very important.

Moving Beyond Conversation and Protesting to Policy Making

While America is often seen as a slavery-free state, there is extensive evidence to show that modern slavery still exists, and it has contributed significantly to racial policing in the country. In 1919, a 17-year-old Black boy was shot by police officers after he swam to what was seen as the wrong part of Lake Michigan. This incident was explained by the segregation laws that existed at the time. Responding to this incident, Black people took to the streets to protest this killing, but White citizens attacked them. There were several other incidences where police officers killed black citizens after this incident. In 1964, segregation laws were abolished, which meant that citizens of color could freely move across the country. This did not, however, stop police from killing innocent Black people. In cases where there were public altercations between White and Black citizens, police officers chose to abet

White mobs and arrest Black people. This notion has not changed to date. Black people are often seen as suspects in a free country, and this explains the increase in cases of police brutality.

There is no doubt that slavery has greatly impacted law enforcement today and contributes massively to racial policing in the country. It is therefore very important to acknowledge the problem and move towards finding suitable solutions. This will go a long way in changing the culture of racial policing and ensuring that all citizens are seen as equal before the law. Further, this will ensure that the country comes to a place of healing from past atrocities that were occasioned by racism. It is further worth noting that dealing with the issues at hand is the only way to ensure that the American dream is realized and actualized.

Figure 83 Black Lives Matter

Black Lives Matter and other racial justice groups have been protesting the killing of Black people as well as other grave injustices and human rights violations that have been prevalent across the U.S. because of racial prejudice. These protests often attract extensive media coverage, with numerous people worldwide joining in the protests for a noble cause. While these protests go a long way in ensuring that the anger and rage of certain people are heard and considered, the major questions that arise are: *"What happens after the protests?" "Are there any systems that are restructured after some of these protests are carried out?"* These and more questions have been asked several times to determine whether the conversation ends with protesting or whether further steps towards policymaking are taken in the end.[191]

The U.S. has, in recent history, experienced remarkable developments amid a pandemic. In a study conducted by the Atlantic, nearly one out of every five Americans are said to have participated in a protest in recent times. This goes to show just how agitated Americans are in the way their social, political, and economic systems are governed. Protections against human rights violations have particularly been on the rise with the increase in police brutality cases against Black people. Therefore, the question is whether protests work and whether the aftermath of these protests is what people often expect.

In answering this question, many scholars who study protests and the impact of protests have been quick to state that protests work. This is often because they are a good way to convey certain concerns among the people involved. There are, however, disclaimers as to how protests work. Scholars have explained that while protests are an effective communication method, they do not work in the way and timeframes that many protestors expect. Protests work both in the short-term and in the long-term. Protests can, for instance, scare authorities and cause the relevant bodies to change their behavior. This is ideally a short-term effect of protests. Protests are an effective way of communicating that protestors and citizens, in general, will not tolerate certain behavior.

It is also worth noting that protests do not always result in immediate corresponding change. The issues that protestors address in some of their matches often take a long time before corresponding policies are put in place and

---

[191] Jennifer Rosa Garcia, "From Protest to Policymaking: Black Legislative Strategies in the Post-War Era" (dissertation, University of California, 2016).

before justice is achieved. A good example would be the case of Cyntoia Brown, a 16-year-old who was convicted of 1st-degree murder for killing a 43-year-old man who was sex trafficking her. While she explained that the murder was a result of self-defense, the jury heard none of these and transferred her to an adult correctional facility. There were protests with people asking authorities to fight against child sex trafficking, but this did not bear any fruit. The girl continued to serve time until the law was revised and put Cyntoia Brown in a position of a child who was being trafficked and not a sex worker who had committed a crime. There are numerous similar cases where protests had not resulted in immediate results but have taken decades before policies and laws were implemented to address the issues in question.

There is a need to move beyond conversation and protesting to policymaking. This is the only way that cases of racial prejudice and discrimination can be addressed effectively. It is further important to note that while protests are a vital method of exercising freedom of speech and an important way to communicate about human rights violations, there is also a need to do more to ensure that citizens are not always protesting over the same things' year-in and year-out. The only way to make this happen is by moving beyond conversations and ensuring that laws are implemented. This will go a long way in providing legal remedies for racial injustice in society.

Protestors often make numerous demands in the course of their protests. On several occasions, protestors have demanded the defunding of police budgets and the abolition of police departments, as well as the development of other institutions that would help keep communities safe. While these are well-thought-out demands aimed at protecting members of the public, they continue to be useless if there are no policies in place to ensure that these demands are implemented.

Figure 84 Defunding of Police Budgets

Demanding that police budgets be reduced significantly as a way of disciplining the police force may not result in an ultimate solution but will instead leave the police operating with limited resources. It is further not enough to invest in social programs that will address violence cases in places prone to police brutality. Having in place policies and implementing laws that help prevent violence against people of color is the way to go. This is the only way to ensure that cases of racial prejudice are dealt with effectively and that justice is realized for the victim and families that lose their loved ones as a result of racial prejudice.[192]

After protests, there is a need to take several pathways beyond mass mobilization. This goes a long way in preventing a repetition of similar scenarios while at the same time increasing awareness of the ongoing issues. While mass protests garner immense local and international attention, the measures taken after these protests are the major determinants of whether a real and lasting change will be achieved. Protests should therefore be used to restructure systems, policies, and social institutions.

Police De-Escalation

Police brutality has been a major cause of violence against people of color. There have been numerous incidents where police officers have been found to use excessive force against citizens. This has given rise to several protests across various states. Police de-escalation is one of the ways through which violence against the citizenry and particularly against people of color can be contained. De-escalation ideally means the strategic slowing down of an incident in a manner that does not result in a violation of human rights. Police can be trained in de-escalation to ensure that they can perform their law enforcement activities appropriately. Some of the de-escalation techniques that can be applied include respect for personal space by the police, being empathetic, avoiding overreacting as well as keeping the legal limits of law enforcement. This will play a significant role in ensuring that cases of police brutality and violence against the public are reduced. De-escalation is not only the responsibility of law enforcement, but people of color must do all in their power to help in fostering de-escalation by complying with police commands. Note that this is a very tall order to ask of a

---

[192] Ryan J. Gallagher and Peter Sheridan Dodds Andrew J. Reagan, Christopher M. Danforth, "Divergent Discourse between Protests and Counter-Protests: #BlackLivesMatter and #AllLivesMatter," PLoS ONE 13, no. 4 (2018): 1–23.

person of color who has been wrongfully mistreated multiple times by the police; however, compliance may be the only option at times to survive.

Funding for Social Projection, Healthcare, And Housing

Racial prejudice and discrimination have taken different forms, including inequalities in health care, housing, and other essential social amenities. For the longest time, these social inequalities have existed, with African Americans who were enslaved over 250 years ago being exposed to miserable social and economic conditions that affected their lives. This resulted in several protests, including people demanding an improvement in Negro health to ensure that it would compare favorably with that of the White race. The end of slavery did not mark the end of miserable health and social conditions among people of color. This group was further exposed to systemic discrimination, and their health systems were inexcusably poor compared to those of their White counterparts.

Although African Americans and people of color represent only about 14% of the U.S. population, they account for the highest percentage of hospital patients in the population. This has often been attributed to a lack of access to high-quality health services, in addition to residential segregation, poverty, violence, and exposure to environments that lack access to healthy foods and safe places to exercise. Numerous steps have been taken to reduce these disparities. The Affordable Care Act is, for instance, one of the tools that seeks to address the special needs of minority groups. This has been done by bringing down health costs for minority groups while, at the same time, supporting improvements in primary care to ensure that minority groups have access to quality health care. Philanthropists have also made significant monetary contributions to ensure that disparities in accessing healthcare services are reduced. Chronic diseases have also been a major issue, particularly for minority groups, given that they are not able to access high-quality and affordable healthcare services. There is a need for reform in healthcare as this is the only way to ensure that racial and ethnic equity in healthcare is achieved.

Structural discrimination in the housing system in the U.S. has also been a major issue for centuries. Issues of displacement, segregation, and exclusion have been prevalent, resulting in poor housing conditions for many minority groups in the U.S. The housing system in the U.S. has been marred with structural racism resulting in social and economic disparities among people of color. For the longest time, African Americans have not had the privilege of homeownership and affordable housing. Minority groups have further not been allowed to acquire property in certain designated neighborhoods, and this has gone a long way to hinder their economic prosperity.[193] There is, therefore, a need to put in place measures and policies aimed at eliminating these inequalities. Having active campaigns against segregation that is based on race is critical to improving social relations and ultimately ensuring that stereotypes against certain groups of people are eliminated.

A long history of systemic racism has kept African Americans from experiencing social and economic stability. This can only be changed by having policy changes that will help improve the social and economic lives of minority groups. Funding for social projections and programming is one of the ways through which this can be realized. This can be done by raising the minimum wages for minority groups, as this would perpetuate improvements in economic conditions. Providing funding to ensure that structural barriers contributing to the high rates of poverty and economic disparities are removed is also very important. Further funding of anti-poverty programs like Medicaid and other social programs will also go a long way in ensuring that economic and racial disparities are eliminated.

---

[193] Lindsay Wells and Arjun Gowda, "A Legacy of Mistrust: African Americans and the US Healthcare System," n.d.

Take Ownership, Learn What It Means to Be Black

The historic election of Barrack Obama as the 44th president of the United States has often been used to describe the U.S. as a post-racial state to mean that there is no more discrimination in the country. Recent events, however, have played a significant role in demising this narrative. Cases of police brutality against members of the Black community and increased tension between minority groups and the authorities have proved otherwise. There are still underlying factors that need to be addressed before declaring the U.S. a racial discrimination-free country. Racial protections that were occasioned by police brutality and the violation of rights of Black people by the police even when they were unarmed speaks a great deal to what it means to be Black in America.

Figure 85 Protesting the Killing of George Floyd

It is worth noting that most of these protests were not about the killings of George Floyd or Breonna Taylor, but rather it is about what it means to be Black in America. Many African Americans have given accounts of their experiences in the U.S. and what they have had to go through because of the color of their skin. Most people explained that their encounters with police officers meant that they were on the edge, even though they had not violated any rules. Others explained that their color played a major role in determining whether they got called for jobs they had applied to, even though they were qualified. Some African Americans have further come out to say that America today is more segregated than it was over 50 years ago. The question therefore is, are any positive steps being taken towards ensuring that the U.S. is racism-free?

While the American dream was meant to empower every American citizen and to ensure that all citizens have equal entitlements, many African Americans have lost faith in the American dream and believe that it is an unrealistic and false dream. Black people further explained that being Black often meant being economically and socially disenfranchised, while White people with lower academic qualifications were being given the upper hand against Black people who were more qualified.

Being Black in America further means being greatly victimized in the criminal justice system. While Black Americans make up only 14% of the population, they contribute to over 33% of the prison population in the U.S. It is further worth noting that an unarmed Black man is more likely to be killed than an armed White man. These discrepancies have been greatly attributed to racial discrimination and deeply rooted institutional racism in the system.

Being Black in America has generally been characterized by struggle and resilience.[194] Many Black people explained that they had to fight historic injustices that contribute to racism up to this day and age. This ideally meant being answerable to the police and being terrorized by law enforcement, even when they had not committed any offenses. Being Black further meant accepting that one would often be treated as a second-class citizen in a country where they paid taxes and contributed to the shaping of social, economic, and political policies.

---

[194] Helen A. Neville and William E. Cross, "Racial Awakening: Epiphanies and Encounters in Black Racial Identity," *Cultural Diversity and Ethnic Minority Psychology* 23, no. 1 (2017): pp. 102-108, https://doi.org/10.1037/cdp0000105.

Taking ownership and learning what it means to be Black in a White-dominated society is very important. It means having an awareness of the surroundings and putting in place measures to ensure that social injustice is eliminated. Learning what it means to be Black further gives a deeper understanding of underlying issues and ways to resolve them. Understanding what it means to be Black also helps individuals to create an action plan and map the way forward on how social, political, and economic injustices that arise as a result can be resolved.

Keep the Dream Alive and Get into "Good Trouble"

The American dream was at one point seen as the only way to bridge the gap between the Whites and Blacks in the American community and ensure that all citizens had similar entitlements. The American dream foresaw a country where children of Black and White members of society would dine together as friends and not shed blood. Years after the launch of this vision by Dr. Martin Luther King, Jr., the American dream remains as such, a dream that is yet to be realized. This is the case following repeated instances of injustice against the Black community and a lack of reasonable accommodation towards minority groups.

Further, the American dream still exists but has taken a new form. Today, the American dream foresees a scenario where every youth can graduate from college, secure a job, afford health and housing benefits, and most importantly, live a comfortable life. This has, however, still not been achieved with many members from minority groups not being able to afford quality affordable housing and health benefits. Many Black men and women have also not been able to graduate college nor secure sustainable jobs, especially because most of them are killed or convicted of petty crimes whenever they have encounters with law enforcement.[195]

---

[195] Péter Perhócs, "Our Kids - on The Book of R. D. Putnam," *Corvinus Journal of Sociology and Social Policy* 7, no. 2 (January 2016): pp. 135-140, https://doi.org/10.14267/cjssp.2016.02.08.

Despite current circumstances, there is hope that the American dream can still be realized. This can, however, only be done by keeping the dream alive and getting into good trouble if it is the only way that this dream will be realized. John Lewis, the iconic congressman, and civil rights activist, at one point, explained that people should never be afraid to make some noise and get into 'good trouble' as this was the only way to achieve social justice in society. In one of his speeches, the legend explained that they were beaten, tear-gassed, and shot at, but they neither gave up nor gave in. They kept the faith and kept their eyes fixed on the prize, as this was the only way to stay focused. On many occasions, he appealed to all those looking for a revolution to get in, to stay in the street of every city and village until true freedom was achieved.

There is a need to keep the dream alive. The dream is that, at some point, all youths, both Black and White, would be treated equally, exposed to equal opportunities, and not be victimized based on the color of their skin. Getting into good trouble would sometimes be joining protests, engaging with law enforcement, and walking across numerous streets to ensure that human rights are not violated and that racial prejudice is eliminated in the country.[196] Persistence is the only way to ensure that the relevant authorities receive the message and that policy measures are put in place to remedy social injustice. It is further important to note that protests are not enough. Citizens need to be brave enough to demand the legislation of certain laws and most importantly, follow through with the implementation of their provisions.

---

[196] Johannes C. Schmid, "Graphic Nonviolence: Framing 'Good Trouble' in John Lewis' March," *European Journal of American Studies*, no. 13-4 (2018), https://doi.org/10.4000/ejas.13922.

BIBLIOGRAPHY

MALOGASSI

Adas, Michael. "A New System of Slavery: The Export of Indian Labour Overseas, 1830–1920. By Hugh Tinker. London: Oxford University Press, 1974. Pp. XVI, 432 + 18 Plates. £5.75." *The Journal of Economic History* 34, no. 4 (1974): 1062–63. https://doi.org/10.1017/s0022050700089695.

Adiante, Franszoon. "The Suriname Maroon Crisis." Cultural Survival Quarterly Magazine. Cultural Survival, December 1, 1988. https://www.culturalsurvival.org/publications/cultural-survival-quarterly/suriname-maroon-crisis.

Adjaye, Joseph K. *Elmina, 'The Little Europe': European Impact and Cultural Resilience.* Sub-Saharan Publishers, 2018.

Agency, Central Intelligence. *The World Factbook 2016-17.* 50th ed. Washington, D.C.: Central Intelligence Agency, 2016.

Alexander, Natasha. *Suriname Country Study Guide.* Washington, DC: International Business Publications, USA, 2005.

Allison Blakely. "Historical Ties among Suriname, the Netherlands Antilles, Aruba, and the Netherlands." *Callaloo* 21, no. 3 (1998): p. 472.

Amersfoort, Hans van. "How the Dutch Government Stimulated the Unwanted Immigration from Suriname." Oxford University Research Archive. University of Oxford, October 2011. ttps://ora.ox.ac.uk/objects/uuid:d71958a0-7fe7-4809-b635-1e468cfb96a1/download_file?file_format=pdf&safe_filename=WP47%2BHow%2Bthe%2BDutch%2BGovernment.pdf&type_of_work=Working+paper.

Archives, The National. "Caribbean Histories Revealed." The National Archives. The National Archives, Kew, Surrey TW9 4DU, November 10, 2006.

https://www.nationalarchives.gov.uk/caribbeanhistory/slavery-negotiating-freedom.htm.

Arends, Jacques. *Language and Slavery: A Social and Linguistic History of the Suriname Creoles.* John Benjamins Pub Co, 2017.

Auty, Richard M. *Natural Resources and Economic Development: Two Stylized Facts Models.* Helsinki, 2000.

Beckles, Hilary McD. "The Slave-Drivers' War: Bussa and the 1816 Barbados Slave Rebellion." *Boletín De Estudios Latinoamericanos Y Del Caribe*, no. 39 (1985): 85–110.

Bilby, Kenneth. "Swearing by the Past, Swearing to the Future: Sacred Oaths, Alliances, and Treaties among the Guianese and Jamaican Maroons." *Ethnohistory* 44, no. 4 (1997): 655–89. https://doi.org/10.2307/482884.

Blakely, Allison. "Historical Ties among Suriname, the Netherlands Antilles, Aruba, and the Netherlands." *Callaloo* 21, no. 3 (1998): 472–78. https://doi.org/10.1353/cal.1998.0135.

"Boni (Ca. 1730 – 1793), Leider Van De Slavenrevoltes in Suriname." IsGeschiedenis, October 9, 2020. https://isgeschiedenis.nl/nieuws/boni-ca-1730-1793-leider-van-de-slavenrevoltes-in-suriname#:~:text=Rond 1780 laaide de strijd, vermoord door Ndjuka-leider Bambi.

Boos, Carla. *De Slavernij. Mensenhandel Van De Koloniale Tijd Tot Nu.* Amsterdam: Balans, 2011.

Borges, Robert. *The Life of Language: Dynamics of Language Contact in Suriname.* Utrecht: LOT, Netherlands Graduate School, 2014.

Brana-Shute, Gary, and Wim Hoogbergen. "The History of the Suriname Maroons." Essay. In *Resistance and Rebellion in Suriname: Old and New*, 65–102. Williamsburg: Dept. of Anthropology, College of William and Mary, 1990.

Bucknor, Beverly. "North American Division Teacher Bulletin." *Teacher Bulletin*. Accessed March 29, 2022. http://www.teacherbulletin.org/media/resources/V01_FullVersion.pdf.

Buddingh, Hans. *Geschiedenis van Suriname (in Dutch)*. Het Spectrum, 1995.

"Caribbean Histories Revealed: Slavery and Negotiating Freedom." *The National Archives*. Last modified 2020. https://www.nationalarchives.gov.uk/caribbeanhistory/slavery-negotiating-freedom.htm.

Carlin, Eithne B. *In and out of Suriname Language, Mobility and Identity*. Leiden, Netherlands: BRILL, 2015.

Carney, Judith A. *Black Rice: The African Origins of Rice Cultivation in the Americas*. Cambridge: Harvard University Press, 2009.

Central Intelligence Agency. Central Intelligence Agency. Accessed March 26, 2022. https://www.cia.gov/the-world-factbook/.

Central Intelligence Agency. *The CIA World Factbook 2011*. New York: Skyhorse Publishing, 2010.

Central Intelligence Agency. *The World Factbook 2016-17. 50th ed.* Washington, D.C.: Central Intelligence Agency, 2016.

Coppens, Bernard. "1815 Malouet." 1789. Accessed March 29, 2022. http://1789-1815.com/p_malouet.htm.

Davies, Carole Boyce. *Encyclopedia of the African Diaspora : Origins, Experiences, and Culture*. ABC-CLIO, 2008.

Dbnl. "DBNL · Digitale Bibliotheek Voor De Nederlandse Letteren." DBNL. Accessed March 28, 2022. https://www.dbnl.org/.

De Groot, Silvia W. "Maroon Women as Ancestors, Priests, and Mediums in Surinam." *Slavery & Abolition* 7, no. 2 (1986): 160–74. https://doi.org/10.1080/01440398608574910.

"Desi Bouterse: Suriname President Gets 20 Years in Jail for Murder." BBC News. BBC, November 30, 2019. https://www.bbc.com/news/world-latin-america-50611555.

Dubelaar, C.N., and André Pakosie. "Kago Buku : Notes by Captain Kago from Tabiki Tapahoni River, Suriname, Written in Afaka Script." *New West Indian Guide / Nieuwe West-Indische Gids* 67, no. 3-4 (1993): 239–79. https://doi.org/10.1163/13822373-90002667.

Dubelaar, C.N., and J.W. Gonggryp. "De Geschriften Van Afaka in Zijn Djoeka-Schrift." *New West Indian Guide / Nieuwe West-Indische Gids* 42, no. 1 (1962): 213–54. https://doi.org/10.1163/22134360-90002324.

"Creole Definition and Meaning: Collins English Dictionary." Creole definition and meaning | Collins English Dictionary. HarperCollins Publishers Ltd. Accessed March 29, 2022. https://www.collinsdictionary.com/dictionary/english/creole.

"Dialect." Cambridge Dictionary. Accessed March 29, 2022. https://dictionary.cambridge.org/grammar/british-grammar/dialect.

Dobbeleir, Céline, Sarrazyn, Jeroen, Van der Straeten, Tineke, Willems, Els, and Van Maele, Pieter. "De Politieke Mobilisatie En Organisatie van Vijf Etnische Groepen in Suriname (PDF). Kennis Bank SU (in Dutch)." University of Gent, n.d. https://kennisbanksu.com/wp-content/uploads/2017/08/de-politieke-mobilisatie-en-organisatie-van-vijf-etnische-groepen-in-Suriname-Universiteit-van-Gent-Maele-Willems-Staete-Sarrazyn-Dobbeleir.pdf.

E., Thoden van Velzen, H. U., W. van Wetering, and Elst Dirk van der. *In the Shadow of the Oracle: Religion as Politics in a Suriname Maroon Society.* Long Grove, IL: Waveland Press, 2004.

Elliott, John H. *Spain, Europe & the Wider World, 1500-1800.* New Haven, CT: Yale University Press, 2009.

Emmer, Pieter. "Between Slavery and Freedom: The Period of Apprenticeship in Suriname (Dutch Guiana), 1863–1873." *Slavery & Abolition* 14, no. 1 (1993): 87–113. https://doi.org/10.1080/01440399308575085.

Emmer, Pieter C. "The History of the Dutch Slave Trade, A Bibliographical Survey." *The Journal of Economic History* 32, no. 3 (1972): 728–47. https://doi.org/10.1017/s0022050700077214.

Esposito, Elena. *Side Effects of Immunities: The African Slave Trade.* Economics Working Papers, 2015.

Fatah-Black, Karwan. "White Lies and Black Markets: Evading Metropolitan Authority in Colonial Suriname, 1650-1800." *The Atlantic World* 31 (2015). https://doi.org/10.1163/9789004283350.

Fetchik, Andrea. *The American Civil Rights Movement.* ACLS Humanities E-Book, 2019. https://www.humanitiesebook.org/the-american-civil-rights-movement/.

Fleury, Marie. "Gaan Mawina, Le Marouini (Haut Maroni) Au Cœur De l'Histoire Des Noirs Marrons Boni/Aluku Et Des Amérindiens Wayana1." *Revue d'ethnoécologie*, no. 13 (2018). https://doi.org/10.4000/ethnoecologie.3534.

Gallagher, Ryan J., Sheridan Dodds, Peter, Reagan, Andrew J., and Danforth, Christopher M. "Divergent Discourse between Protests and Counter-Protests: #BlackLivesMatter and #AllLivesMatter." *PLoS ONE* 13, no. 4 (2018): 1–23.

Garcia, Jennifer Rosa. "From Protest to Policymaking: Black Legislative Strategies in the Post-War Era." Dissertation, University of California, 2016.

Gates, Henry Louis, and Evelyn Brooks Higginbotham. *African American Lives.* New York: Oxford University Press, 2004.

"Genetic Impact of African Slave Trade Revealed in DNA Study." BBC News. BBC, July 24, 2020. https://www.bbc.com/news/world-africa-53527405.

Glass, Andrew. "Barack Obama Elected 44th U.S. President, Nov. 4, 2008." POLITICO, November 4, 2011. https://www.politico.com/story/2013/11/barack-obama-elected-44th-us-president-nov-4-2008-099280.

Gomes da Cunha, Olivia Maria, Kenneth Bilby, and Rivke Jaffe. "'Real Bushinengué': Guianese Maroon Music in Transition." Essay. In *Maroon Cosmopolitics: Personhood, Creativity and Incorporation*, 330–49. Leiden: Brill, 2019.

Griffith, Ivelaw L. *The Re-Emergence of Suriname's Désiré (DESI) Bouterse: Political Acumen and Geopolitical Anxiety*. Miami, FL: Applied Research Center, Florida International University, 2011.

Groot, Silvia Wilhelmina. "Rebellie Der Zwarte Jagers: De Nasleep Van De Bonni-Oorlogen 1788-1809." *The Guide*, 1970. https://dbnl.nl/tekst/_gid001197001_01/_gid001197001_01_0083.php?q=Re bellie der Zwarte Jagers. De nasleep van de Bonni-oorlogen.

Gupta, Das Tania, and Verene Shepherd. "Prelude to Settlement: Indians as Indentured Labourers." Essay. In *Race and Racialization: Essential Readings*, 155–56. Toronto: Canadian Scholars, 2018.

"Haitian Revolution: Haitian History." *Brittanica Encyclopedia*. Last modified 2021. https://www.britannica.com/topic/Haitian-Revolution.

Heuman, Gad J. *Out of the House of Bondage: Runaways, Resistance and Marronage in Africa and the New World*. London: Routledge, 2016.

Heuman, Gad J. "Riots and Resistance in the Caribbean at the Moment of Freedom." *Slavery & Abolition* 21, no. 2 (2000): 135–49. https://doi.org/10.1080/01440390008575309.

"History of Suriname." Encyclopædia Britannica. Encyclopædia Britannica, inc. Accessed March 28, 2022. https://www.britannica.com/place/Suriname/History.

"History of the Caribbean Community." CARICOM, July 23, 2020. https://caricom.org/history-of-the-caribbean-community/.

Hoefte, Rosemarijn. "A Passage to Suriname? The Migration of Modes of Resistance by Asian Contract Laborers." *International Labor and Working-Class History* 54 (1998): 19–39. https://doi.org/10.1017/s0147547900006190.

Hoefte, Rosemarijn. "Control and Resistance: Indentured Labor in Suriname." *New West Indian Guide/Nieuwe West-Indische Gids* 61, no. 1-2 (1987): 1–22. https://doi.org/10.1163/13822373-90002053.

Hoefte, Rosemarijn. "Free Blacks and Coloureds in Plantation Suriname." *Slavery & Abolition* 17, no. 1 (1996): 102–29. https://doi.org/10.1080/01440399608575178.

Hoffman, Bruce. "Exploring Biocultural Contexts: Comparative Woody Plant Knowledge of an Indigenous and Afro-American Maroon Community in Suriname, South America." *African Ethnobotany in the Americas*, 2012, 335–93. https://doi.org/10.1007/978-1-4614-0836-9_13.

Hoogbergen, Wim, and Dirk Kruijt. "Gold, 'Garimpeiros' and Maroons: Brazilian Migrants and ..." Caribbean Studies. Institute of Caribbean Studies, 2004. https://www.jstor.org/stable/25613440.

Hoogbergen, Wim. "Origins of the Suriname Kwinti Maroons." *New West Indian Guide / Nieuwe West-Indische Gids* 66, no. 1-2 (1992): 27–59. https://doi.org/10.1163/13822373-90002003.

Howard, Rosalyn. "'Looking For Angola': An Archaeological and Ethnohistorical Search for a Nineteenth-Century Florida Maroon Community and Its

Caribbean Connections." *The Florida Historical Quarterly* 92, no. 1 (2013): 32–68. http://www.jstor.org/stable/43487549.

Huzzey, Richard. *Freedom Burning: Anti-Slavery and Empire in Victorian Britain*. Ithaca: Cornell University Press, 2012.

Jamison, David. "From Resistance to Marronage: Slave Networks and the Forging of Identity in the Dutch Guianas, 1763--1823." Dissertation, ProQuest Dissertations Publishing, 2014.

Jones, Jacqueline, and M. H. Jung. "Outlawing 'Coolies': Race, Nation, and Empire in the Age of Emancipation." Essay. In *The Best American History Essays 2007*, 111–33. Palgrave Macmillan, 2007.

Kaplan, Sidney. "Jan Earnst Matzeliger and the Making of the Shoe." *The Journal of Negro History* 40, no. 1 (1955): 8–33. https://doi.org/10.2307/2715446.

Koene, Bert. *De Mensen Van Vossenburg En Wayampibo: Twee Surinaamse Plantages in De Slaventijd*. Hilversum: Verloren, 2019.

"Kwasimukamba's Gambit." Bijdragen Tot de Taal-, Land-En Volkenkunde." *Journal of the Humanities and Social Sciences of Southeast Asia* 135, no. 1 (1979): 151–169.

Lamur, Humphrey. "The Impact of Maroon Wars on Population Policy during Slavery in Suriname." *Journal of Caribbean History* 23, no. 1 (1989): 1.

Lotzof, Kerry. "Who Was Graman Kwasi?" Natural History Museum. Accessed March 29, 2022. https://www.nhm.ac.uk/discover/who-was-graman-kwasi.html.

Léglise, Isabelle, and Bettina Migge. "Language-Naming Practices, Ideologies, and Linguistic Practices: Toward a Comprehensive Description of Language Varieties." *Language in Society* 35, no. 03 (2006): 313–39. https://doi.org/10.1017/s0047404506060155.

MacDonald, Scott B. "Insurrection and Redemocratization in Suriname? The Ascendancy of the 'Third Path.'" *Journal of Interamerican Studies and World Affairs* 30, no. 1 (1988): 105–32. https://doi.org/10.2307/165791.

MacDonald, Scott B. "Suriname's Economic Crisis." Center for Strategic and International Studies, April 20, 2017. https://www.csis.org/analysis/surinames-economic-crisis.

Meijer, Miriam Claude, and Petrus Camper. "History of Anthropology Newsletter." *Penn Libraries*, January 1997. https://repository.upenn.edu/han/vol24/iss2/3.

Menke, Jack. "The Political Culture of Democracy in Suriname and in the Americas, 2012: Towards Equality of Opportunity, 2013." *USAID from the American People*, June 2013.

Migge, Bettina. "Code-Switching and Social Identities in the Eastern Maroon Community of Suriname and French Guiana." *Journal of Sociolinguistics* 11, no. 1 (2007): 53–73. https://doi.org/10.1111/j.1467-9841.2007.00310.x.

Minchinton, Walter. "The Dutch in the Atlantic Slave Trade: 1600-1815." *The English Historical Review* 109, no. 431 (1994): 454+. *Gale Literature Resource Center* (accessed March 21, 2022) Misiedjan, Martin. "The Ndyuka Treaty Of 1760: A Conversation with Granman Gazon." *Cultural Survival*, December 2001. https://www.culturalsurvival.org/publications/cultural-survival-quarterly/ndyuka-treaty-1760-conversation-granman-gazon.

Minchinton, Walter. "The End of the Dutch Slave Trade, 1781–1815." *The English Historical Review* 109, no. 431 (1994): 454–54. https://doi.org/10.1017/cbo9780511528958.013.

Misiedjan, Martin. "The Ndyuka Treaty of 1760: A Conversation with Granman Gazon." Cultural Survival, December 1, 2001. https://www.culturalsurvival.org/publications/cultural-survival-quarterly/ndyuka-treaty-1760-conversation-granman-gazon.

Monsels, D.A. "Bauxite Deposits in Suriname: Geological Context and Resource Development: Netherlands Journal of Geosciences." Cambridge Core. Cambridge University Press, March 17, 2016. https://core-cms.prod.aop.cambridge.org/core/journals/netherlands-journal-of-geosciences/article/bauxite-deposits-in-suriname-geological-context-and-resource-development/CF28E3F7ECAA5BA0EBCC34334CDEF257.

Moore, Bob, and Nierop Henk F K van. Essay. In *Colonial Empires Compared: Britain and the Netherlands, 1750-1850: Papers Delivered to the Fourteenth Anglo-Dutch Historical Conference, 2000.* Aldershot, Hampshire, England: Ashgate, 2003.

"MPM Collection." Milwaukee Public Museum. Accessed March 27, 2022. https://www.mpm.edu/research-collections/anthropology/online-collections-research/ndyuka/mpm-collection.

Nations, United. *Preliminary Overview of the Economies of Latin America and the Caribbean 2017.* Washington D.C.: United Nations Economic Commission for Latin America and the Caribbean, 2018.

"Ndyuka." Ethnologue. Accessed March 27, 2022. https://www.ethnologue.com/subgroups/suriname.

"Ndyuka." *Encyclopedia.Com.* Last modified 2021. https://www.encyclopedia.com/humanities/encyclopedias-almanacs-transcripts-and-maps/ndyuka.

Neville, Helen A., and William E. Cross. "Racial Awakening: Epiphanies and Encounters in Black Racial Identity." *Cultural Diversity and Ethnic Minority Psychology* 23, no. 1 (2017): 102–8. https://doi.org/10.1037/cdp0000105.

Oats, Lynne, Sadler, Pauline, and Wynter, Carlene. "Taxing Jamaica: The Stamp Act of 1760 & Tacky's Rebellion." *eJournal of Tax Research* 12, no. 1 (2014): pp. 162–184.

Oostindie, Gert. "Voltaire, Stedman and Suriname Slavery." *Slavery & Abolition* 14, no. 2 (1993): 1–34. https://doi.org/10.1080/01440399308575095.

Pakosie, André R.M. "Maroon Leadership and the Surinamese State (1760–1990)." *The Journal of Legal Pluralism and Unofficial Law* 28, no. 37-38 (1996): 263–77. https://doi.org/10.1080/07329113.1996.10756483.

Paxton, John. *The Statesman's Yearbook: Statistical and Historical Annual of the States of the World for the Year*. London: Macmillan, 1976.

Perhócs, Péter. "Our Kids - on The Book of r. d. Putnam." *Corvinus Journal of Sociology and Social Policy* 7, no. 2 (2016): 135–40. https://doi.org/10.14267/cjssp.2016.02.08.

Postma, Johannes. *The Dutch in the Atlantic Slave Trade, 1600-1815*. Cambridge: Cambridge Univ. Press, 2008.

Price, Richard. "Executing Ethnicity: The Killings in Suriname." *Cultural Anthropology* 10, no. 4 (1995): 437–71. https://doi.org/10.1525/can.1995.10.4.02a00010.

Price, Richard. "Kwasimukamba's Gambit." *Bijdragen tot de taal-, land- en volkenkunde / Journal of the Humanities and Social Sciences of Southeast Asia* 135, no. 1 (1979): 151–69. https://doi.org/10.1163/22134379-90002574.

Reckord, Mary. "The Jamaica Slave Rebellion of 1831." *Past & Present*, no. 40 (1968): 108–25.

Rice, Alan. "Revealing Histories: Remembering Slavery." Legacies of slavery: dance | Revealing Histories. Accessed March 27, 2022. http://revealinghistories.org.uk/legacies-stereotypes-racism-and-the-civil-rights-movement/articles/legacies-of-slavery-dance.html.

Rice, Alan. "Riots and Resistance in the Caribbean at the Moment of Freedom." *Slavery & Abolition* 21, no. 2 (2000): 135–149.

Rodriguez, Junius P. *Encyclopedia of Emancipation and Abolition in the Transatlantic World.* Armonk, NY: M.E. Sharpe, 2007.

Rubenstein, Anne, Camilla Townsend, and Christopher Z. Hobson. "Revolted Negroes and the Devilish Principle: William Blake and Conflicting Visions of Boni's Wars in Surinam, 1772–1796." *Blake, Politics, and History,* 2015, 273–98. https://doi.org/10.4324/9781315675176-16.

Ryden, David B. "Revolutionary Emancipation: Slavery and Abolitionism in the British West Indies, Written by Claudius K. Fergus." *New West Indian Guide* 90, no. 1-2 (2016): 86–88. https://doi.org/10.1163/22134360-09001004.

Sawh, Ruth, and Scales, Alice M. "Middle Passage in the Triangular Slave Trade: The West Indies." *Negro Educational Review* 57, no. 3/4 (2006): 155–170.

Schiebinger, Londa L. *Plants and Empire: Colonial Bioprospecting in the Atlantic World.* Cambridge, MA: Harvard University Press, 2007.

Schiebinger, Londa. *Secret Cures of Slaves: People, Plants, and Medicine in the Eighteenth-Century Atlantic World.* Stanford: Stanford University Press, 2017.

Schmid, Johannes C. "Graphic Nonviolence: Framing 'Good Trouble' in John Lewis's March." *European Journal of American studies,* no. 13-4 (2018). https://doi.org/10.4000/ejas.13922.

Scholtens, Ben. "Bosnegers En Overheid in Suriname: De Ontwikkeling van de Politieke Verhouding 1651-1992." *New West Indian Guide / Nieuwe West-Indische Gids* 70, no. 1/2 (1996): 199–201.

Sharpe, Jenny. *Ghosts of Slavery: A Literary Archaeology of Black Women's Lives.* Minneapolis, MN: Univ. of Minnesota Press, 2003.

Shepherd, Verene. "Prelude to Settlement: Indians as Indentured Labourers." In *Race and Racialization: Essential Readings*, 155, 2007.

Sherwood, Marika. *After Abolition: Britain and the Slave Trade since 1807*. London: I.B. Tauris, 2007.

Smith, Raymond T. *Negro Family in British Guiana: Family Structure and Social Status in the Villages*. New York, NY: Routledge, 2013.

Spence, Caroline Quarrier. "Ameliorating Empire: Slavery and Protection in the British Colonies, 1783-1865." Harvard University, 2014.

Stedman, John Gabriel, William Blake, and Francesco Bartolozzi. *Narrative, of a Five Years' Expedition, against the Revolted Negroes of Surinam, in Guiana, on the Wild Coast of South America, from the Year 1772 to 1777: Elucidating the History of That Country and Describing Its Productions ... with an Account of the Indians of Guiana, & Negroes of Guinea*. London: Printed for J. Johnson ... & J. Edwards, 1796.

Stipriaan, Alex Van. "In and Out of Suriname: Language, Mobility and Identity." In *Maroons and the Communications Revolution in Suriname's Interior*, edited by Eithne B. Carlin, Isabelle Léglise, Bettina Migge, and Paul Brendan Tjon Sie Fat, 139–163. Leiden: BRILL, 2015.

"Suriname Country Profile." BBC News. BBC, March 3, 2021. https://www.bbc.com/news/world-latin-america-19997673.

"Suriname." Visit the main page. Accessed March 28, 2022. https://www.newworldencyclopedia.org/entry/Suriname.

"Suriname's Economic Crisis." Center for Strategic and International Studies, April 2017. Accessed February 22, 2019. https://www.csis.org/analysis/surinames-economic-crisis.

Temperley, Howard, ed. *After Slavery: Emancipation and Its Discontents*. Portland, OR: Frank Cass, 2000.

"The History of the Dutch Slave Trade, A Bibliographical Survey." *The Journal of Economic History* 32, no. 3 (1972): 728–747.

"The History of the Suriname Maroons." In *Resistance and Rebellion in Suriname : Old and New,* edited by Gary Brana-Shute, 65–102. Williamsburg, VA: College of William and Mary, 1990.

Timpson, Thomas. *The Negroes' Jubilee: A Memorial of Negro Emancipation, August 1, 1834: With a Brief History of the Slave Trade and Its Abolition, and the Extinction of British Colonial Slavery.* London: Ward and Co., 1834.

Titley, Gavan, and John Wrench. "Managing Diversity, Fighting Racism or Combating Discrimination? A Critical Exploration." Essay. In *Resituating Culture,* 113–33. Strasbourg Cedex: Council of Europe Pub., 2004.

Twaddle, Michael, ed. *The Wages of Slavery: From Chattel Slavery to Wage Labour in Africa, the Caribbean, and England.* London: Routledge, 2015.

Van der Linden, Marcel. "The Okanisi: A Surinamese Maroon Community, C.1712–2010." *International Review of Social History* 60, no. 3 (2015): 463–90. https://doi.org/10.1017/s0020859015000383.

Van Maele , Pieter. "Op Zoek Naar Fort Boekoe." Trouw, September 7, 2012. https://www.trouw.nl/nieuws/op-zoek-naar-fort-boekoe~bfd676d4/?referrer=https%3A%2F%2Fwww.google.com%2F.

Van Velzen, Wilhelmina, and H.U.E. Thoden van Velzen. "Suriname: Een Wingewest Van De Republiek." *Een zwarte vrijstaat in Suriname (deel 2),* Caribbean Series, no. 32 (2013): 53–64. https://doi.org/10.1163/9789004255494_004.

Velzen, H. U. E. Thoden Van, Wetering, Ineke Van, Wetering, W. Van, and Der Elst, Dirk Van. *In the Shadow of the Oracle: Religion As Politics in a Suriname Maroon Society.* Waveland Press Inc, 2004.

Wells, Lindsay, and Arjun Gowda. "Proceedings of UCLA Health," 2020.

Wharton, David Eugene. *The Engineering and Technological Education of Black Americans: 1865-1950*. Amherst, MA: University of Massachusetts Amherst, 2019.

Williamson, Joel. *After Slavery: The Negro in South Carolina during Reconstruction, 1861-1877*. Chapel Hill, NC: University of North Carolina Press, 1965.

Wright, Philip. "War and Peace with the Maroons, 1730–1739." *Caribbean Quarterly* 16, no. 1 (1970): 5–27. https://doi.org/10.1080/00086495.1970.11829035.

Wright, Philip. "War and Peace with the Maroons, 1730–1739." *Caribbean Quarterly* 16, no. 1 (1970): 5–27.

Yakpo, Kofi, and Robert Borges. "The Maroon Creoles of the Guianas: Expansion, Contact, and Hybridization." Essay. In *Boundaries and Bridges: Language Contact in Multilingual Ecologies*, 87–128. Boston: Walter de Gruyter, 2017.

PAGE DEDICATION

I would like to bestow a special thanks to my dissertation chair, Dr. Ava E. Carroll, Administrator of Online Learning Systems at New York Theological Seminary, for lending her expertise and time to the formulation of my visionary works during my doctoral journey. Thank you for your countless hours of reading, reflections, encouragement (even threatening to "kick my butt!"), and feedback that created a spirit of adventure and anticipation during my ancestral history and cultural identity quest. Your thirst for knowledge and understanding has contributed to the expanded work seen here today.